FEVER, FAMINE, AND GOLD

Author

CAPTAIN E. ERSKINE LOCH, D.S.O.

FEVER FAMINE AND GOLD

The Dramatic Story of the Adventures and Discoveries of the Andes-Amazon Expedition in the Uncharted Fastnesses of a Lost World in the Llanganatis Mountains.

G · P · PUTNAM'S SONS

NEW YORK

A PATHFINDER BOOK REPRINT EDITION
Complete and Unabridged

Printed in the United States of America

ISBN: 979-8-8691-1411-2

TO

THE MEMORY OF

PRIVATE JOSÉ PONS

SOMETIME SOLDIER

OF THE

MONTUFAR BATTALION

ECUADOREAN ARMY

Contents

APPENDICES

Illustrations

MAPS

Introduction

A FEW YEARS AGO the public's ever-increasing demand for thrills forced explorers, often against their will, to give accounts of their explorations that far exceeded their rightful field of truth. Breath-taking escapes and adventures were demanded. Then came a new fashion, that of burlesquing exploration and its risks.

It became the mode to return from a trip with stories of having fondled a rhinoceros much as one would a pekinese and of having fed a lion out of the back of one's car with a ham sandwich or two.

I trust there still remains the simple middle course. In the narrative of this Expedition I have deliberately shortened a few wearisome lapses of time, and have attempted to minimize the necessarily repetitious accounts of daily routine scientific work and mechanical details in favor of those features of more general interest which we pursued. And in the last chapter I have intentionally withheld the names of two men and of a place for obvious reasons.

Before leaving New York it had appeared to me, from rumors and conjectures, that the Curaray River had a winding course and that there was only a small difference in altitude between its headwaters and the frontier. These were indications that it might be free from rapids or falls. If so, I saw no reason why it should not prove to be a safe, navigable waterway right through the Oriente to the frontier. A direct passage then, through the Llanganatis Mountains, from the railroad to the source of the Curaray, with a link to Napo Town, was a logical counterpart; and it was searching for these two things that linked together the whole year and four months of the Expedition's work.

So little was known about either region that each offered an extremely interesting field for research. Also the itinerary as finally laid out was to take us through an area cloaked with one of the most colorful and romantic stories in the history of South America.

But I trust that no story of a famous treasure is too alluring to overshadow the other work we did. In all justice to George Brun, John Ohman, and Wilfried Klamroth, Jr., all of whom toiled endlessly in the service of the Expedition, I wish to say that we brought back many thousands of observations, thermometric and hygrometic readings, ethnological and natural history specimens, which are now in leading institutions in New York, Chicago, Philadelphia, and Great Britain. Such things require constant daily work, arduous and uninspiring, and, under conditions in the field, are most difficult to acquire.

The scientist, most understandably, does not as a rule care to associate himself with romance, lost treasures, and so forth. Personally, I have no such qualms. But then, I am not a scientist and make no pretensions whatsoever to being one. I'm a British Army Officer, retired, who does things for the love of them, that's all. But a life of travel takes me to far-off places from which I bring back such information as I can.

Not one single man of us took any part at all in South American politics, nor have we any bias whatever on that score. Any service that our records may contribute towards the Ecuador of the future is given purely out of affection for that country.

Although months have now passed since those turbulent days spent in the Llanganatis Mountains and the Oriente, to me they seem but as yesterday. For at the very moment this book goes to press, the New York newspapers are carrying dispatches of another clash on the Ecuador-Peru frontier, involving people and places directly connected with this Expedition. It was through Rocafuerte, the main garrison on the frontier, and Tarqui, the military post on the Curaray, that the Expedition journeyed.

I regret that it was impossible to record photographically the more exciting happenings of the Expedition. In the Llanganatis Mountains the constant clouds, rain, and fog rendered picture-making an all but impossible task.

I wish to express my gratitude to all those in the United States and Ecuador who assisted the Expedition, and to thank Mr. Alfred Batson for his help in editing and preparing this manuscript.

E. Erskine Loch

Explorer's Club
New York, June, 1938

FEVER, FAMINE, AND GOLD

Chapter I
THE LOST TREASURE OF VALVERDE

IT WAS THE spring of 1935. As I emerged from the New York Public Library, my mind was aflame with the few startling pages of history I had just been reading. The Valverde Treasure! The Lost Mines of the Incas! The Legend of the Llanganatis Mountains of Ecuador! The story stood before me like a beacon. What hidden mysteries, what vast hoards of gold might be secreted in those distant, snowy peaks! Just four hundred years earlier Spain had conquered that mighty Empire of the Incas.

I continued on up Fifth Avenue. "Roosevelt and the Gold Standard!" "High Price of Gold!" The bold headlines struck the eye at every corner. But what irony! The Incas, whose gold, flooding Europe, was a potent factor in *putting the world on the gold standard*, had never used gold as money. They had no monetary system. How happy they were without it! They had *no* word for "rich" or "poor," and not a pauper in their land!

A vision of that Empire's tragic end sprang up before my mind, and on that instant came a desire—a sudden determination to reach those far-off Llanganatis, and find a short route to the Amazon.

Uncharted territory, rare animals, a tribe of Indians of which little or nothing was known, and a region which offered abundant fields for exploration and research! And with it all, that slender fabric of an ancient legend—hidden lakes, lost treasure, Llanganatis Gold!

Ethnological, geographical, and other scientific purposes soon took root as my plans developed. In fact they were soon an obligation on my part, for Mr. Heye, Director of the Museum of the American Indian (Heye Foundation), of New York, knowing the scientific value of the region, placed me under that institution's auspices for ethnological research.

Hectic weeks of turmoil followed. Boxes, bales, equipment, men—all crowded through the panorama of those busy days.

The summer came. By August we were ready. The Andes-Amazon Expedition was organized, and on its way to South America.

Carl de Muralt, tall, slender, second in command of the Expedition, raised his eyes from the book for the first time since leaving Guayaquil—but not to watch the banana plantations and orange groves, or glance back at the ship we had so recently left. He was oblivious to all that surrounded him. Perspiration ran down his determined face, but he wore a look of sublime indifference to the dust, flies, and general discomfort of the airless coach as we rocked and jolted along on the first stage from sea level to the high altitude of Riobamba.

I knew what was going on in his mind. It had been building up ever since that day months before in New York when we'd met under such unusual circumstances. He was as enthusiastic as I.

"... The Valverde Guide!" Carl said. "The Guide to the Treasure!"

The others sat forward—John Ohman, the radio engineer, Le Grand (Sonny) Griswold, much-traveled New Yorker, who had come for new adventure and was now blithely forgetting the blistering heat of Ecuador with a blood-curdling yarn laid in Greenland, and the Parisian George Brun, ex-aviator, ballistics enthusiast, and good hunter. Other appointments being filled, he had joined as supply and transport officer.

"The lost mines of the Incas," said Carl.

"Lost for four hundred years," I put in.

"Yes," Carl rejoined, "but Valverde found them— why shouldn't we? I'll sketch the background briefly."

Everyone was listening—

"At the time of the Conquest a poor Spanish soldier named Valverde married an Inca woman, whose father vowed to make his new son-in-law the richest of all Conquistadores. This he proceeded to do by leading him across the Llanganatis Mountains to a hoard of gold. It was Incan, or pre-Incan, treasure and was in the unknown 'Oriente' district deep in the interior. How much gold Valverde got, no one knows. But history states that from being an impecunious soldier he became overnight a very wealthy man. When he died he left a paper of detailed instructions known as the Guide, or 'Derrotero,' which he willed to the King of Spain. The King subsequently sent an expedition to find the cache but without success—"

"It has been so ever since," I interrupted. "Search after search has led to such disasters that the region has now become shrouded in superstition and almost a land of legend. As late as 1912 an American, Colonel E. C. Brooks, went in looking for the treasure. He followed the 'Derrotero' closely but was flooded out by a cloudburst, deserted by his Indians, and when eventually rescued by a searching party was wandering in the mountains practically out of his mind, and died not long afterwards in New York—he was only one."

Carl nodded in agreement, but, undeterred, he turned again to his book. "Listen! the Guide reads:

Placed in the town of Pillaro, ask for the farm of Moya and sleep the first night a good distance above and ask there for the mountain of Guapa, from whose top, if the day be fine, look to the East, so that thy back be towards the town of Ambato, and from thence thou shalt perceive the three Cerros Llanganati, in the form of a triangle, on whose declivity is a lake, made by hand, into which the ancients cast the gold they had prepared for the ransom of the Inca when they heard of his death."

John was deeply interested. Griswold had so far forgotten Greenland as to be listening intently; and George Brun, though a bit skeptical, was tugging at the lobe of his ear.

I held my peace and waited; for I knew the "Valverde Treasure Guide," copied from the ancient archives of Madrid, almost by heart; and at my own first reading of the detailed instructions for finding the treasure I had been as enthralled as those around me now. But, as time went on, I, like Carl, had come to know the hidden contradictions contained in that Guide—pitfalls that were not at once apparent at first reading and that were no less disheartening when met with on the scene.

"...from this same Cerro Guapa thou mayst see also the forest, and in it a clump of sangurimas standing out of the said forest, and another clump which they call flechas, and these clumps are the principal marks for which thou shalt aim, leaving them a little to the left hand. Go forward from Guapa in this direction and with the signals indicated, and a good way ahead, having passed some cattle farms, thou shalt come upon a wild morass over which thou must cross, and coming on the other side thou shalt see upon they left hand a short way off a jucal upon a hillside, through which thou must pass..."

This was all right for Carl, who had come along mainly to seek the treasure and was to lead a separate party; but, fascinated as I was with the subject, I was operating under the auspices of the Museum and had definite scientific obligations to fulfill first, from which in this early stage I could not afford to be swerved. I had to create a diversion; so, ostentatiously, I reached in my bag and brought out a batch of papers—

"We need ethnological and anthropological data for the Museum on the Zaparo Indians of the Curaray River. It is a populous tribe and said to be friendly—"

No one was listening.

"...having gone through the jucal thou wilt see two small lakes known as Los Anteojos from having betwixt them a point of land like unto a nose. From this place thou mayst again see the Cerros Llanganati, the same as thou sawest from the top of Cerro Guapa, and I warn thee to leave the said Lakes on thy left, and that in front of the point, or nose, there is a plain which is thy sleeping place. There thou must leave the horses, for they can go no farther. Following now on foot in the same direction, thou shalt come upon a great black lake, which leave on thy left hand, and beyond it seek to descend along the hillside in such manner that thou mayst reach a quebrada [ravine] down which comes a waterfall; and here thou shalt find a bridge of three poles, or if it do not still exist, place another in the most convenient place and so pass over..."

"The Museum of Natural History wants a specimen of the *anteojos,* or 'spectacled bear.'" Again I was talking to myself.

"...and having gone a little way in the forest beyond, seek out the hut which served to sleep in or the remains thereof. Having passed the night here, go on thy way through the forest in the same direction till thou reachest another deep dry ravine across which thou must throw a bridge, and pass over it slowly and cautiously, for the quebrada is very deep; that is, if thou succeeded not in finding the pass which exists. Go forward and look for signs of another sleeping place, which I assure thee thou canst not fail to see in the fragments of pottery and other marks, because the Indians are continually passing that way. Go now on thy way and thou shalt see a mountain which is all of margasitas [pyrites], the which leave on thy left hand, and I warn thee thou must go around it in this fashion..." (here follows a hieroglyphic.—E. E. L.).

"Another animal found only in these high Andes is the hairy tapir, very rare and quite different from the tapir of the lowlands. The New York Zoological Society—"

"...on this side thou shalt find a pajonal [pasture] in a small plain, which having been crossed, thou wilt come on a cañon betwixt two hills which is the Way of the Inca. From thence as thou goest thou shalt see the entrance to the socabon [tunnel], which is in the form of a church porch. Having come through the cañon and gone a goodly distance beyond, thou shalt perceive a cascade which descends from an offshoot of Cerros Llanganati and runs into a quaking bog on thy right hand. Without passing this said bog there is much gold..."

"Let's hurry!" came from Griswold. "Washington is buying gold at a premium—"

I broke in again, but I might as well have been talking to the moon. Carl rushed on.

"...so that by putting in thy hand what thou shalt gather at the bottom is grains of gold. To ascend the mountain, leave the bog and go along to the right and pass above the cascade, going around the offshoot of the mountain. If by chance the mouth of the tunnel be closed by certain herbs, remove them and thou shalt find the entrance. And on the left hand side of the mountain thou mayst see the guayra (for thus the ancients called the furnace wherein they founded metals) which is nailed with golden nails. And to reach the third mountain, if thou canst not pass in front of the socabon, it is the same thing to pass behind it, for the water from the lake falls into it."

"Then if it is in a lake, why hasn't someone found it?" George Brun asked.

"There are about a hundred lakes on the best maps available," I said, "and many more that aren't even known about—at least that's my experience with South American maps. But whether it's a treasure in a lake, a mine, or both, four hundred years of searching leaves it anybody's guess."

The whole matter was indeed one of great interest, which in the back of my mind subtly exerted its centuries-old magic upon me as much as upon the others. It had been taken very seriously by such recognized authorities as Richard Spruce and Hassaurek, who had given much thought and study to the matter. The original Guide sent to Ecuador by the King of Spain contained old Spanish phraseology, obsolete words, and terms capable of being interpreted in various ways; but, because of the wealth to which it refers, it is one of the best-known treasure stories in the world today. To prove or disprove the legend of the Lost Mines or Treasure—and one should lead to the other—was a matter of legitimate historical interest and one which wanted dealing with later as soon as opportunity offered.

For the first time since leaving Guayaquil the others now began showing an interest in the passing countryside as the train jerked and panted away from the lowlands, thundering over ravines innumerable, zigzagging and staggering and never relinquishing an inch. It was a region of nondescript habitations with the inevitable chickens and goats, scrawny beyond anything we'd seen back in the States.

But a few hours later, when we'd crested the top of the pass, we entered a broad expanse of open, desolate country—the first indication of what lay ahead.

John busied himself with the financial accounts of

the Expedition, a job he had assumed entirely of his own volition, and one of which I was happy to be rid. Before leaving New York a last-minute decision to take radio equipment with us had made me send out a call, at our request, over the Amateur Radio Relay League network. John volunteered. Within the few days that remained he had built his own set, both transmitter and receiver, over which we sent and received many thousands of words between New York and many parts of Ecuador. His ability to handle instruments brought a multitude of jobs upon his shoulders, each one of which he carried out with equal efficiency. John has no guile nor deceit in his character, and it was typical of him that one day when I was wrestling with my checkbook by that excellent method of starting at the balance, which after all is what matters, and filling out the stubs from memory and guess work, he looked over my shoulder and said sternly, "Captain, that's not honest."

"But if I'm cheating anyone it's only myself," I reminded him somewhat stiffly.

"No matter," he said, "it's not honest."

That was John Ohman.

George Brun was but a few years older. Of nerves he had none; on the contrary, he was full of undaunted courage and was of considerable initiative. Weighing some ninety-odd pounds from his appearance, *looking* desperately delicate, as he did, he was warned by his doctor before leaving New York that he could not last six months with the Expedition. He went through every turbulent day of it and is still more than ready to do it all over again! The possessor of numerous medals for marksmanship, most of the Expedition's natural history specimens fell to his rifle. I was never to regret my choice of George.

A dozen expeditions in India, Africa, and South America, eleven years as a British Army Officer in various campaigns have taught me the wisdom of choosing men for themselves and because of certain traits of character often indiscernible by the eye or ear, rather than by a long list of professed abilities. I have seen veteran soldiers become panic-stricken at meeting a situation not in the book of instructions; and, conversely, I have known untutored and untried men to face emergencies and conquer them through a sudden spark of leadership or initiative that springs up within themselves. What man knows how he will act under the stress of sudden crisis?

We had outfitted ourselves for eight months with the variegated supplies and clothing necessary to penetrate not only the windswept, chilling Andean heights but also the extreme opposite, the festering, malaria-filled swamplands of the Upper Curaray. In addition, Carl de Muralt had brought along a complete outfit for prospecting and mining, which, together with our personal belongings, made up one hundred and eight pieces of baggage.

It was two expeditions in one and, unlike others which have a single objective in view, its aims were many and diverse.

By late afternoon we had begun descending out of the higher altitudes; suddenly the ground spread open before us like a gigantic bowl, in the center of which stood a small cluster of miniature houses against a background so fantastic as to make one catch his breath. Mighty Chimborazo and Altar stretched their white-capped peaks into the infinite blue; and, in contrast to their majestic splendor, between them lay the little town of Riobamba, like a tiny jewel in a setting beyond the ability of man to conceive.

The sun had almost sunk behind the lofty cordilleras. Beyond us towered the Peaks of Llanganati, grim and forbidding, guarding in their fastnesses an age-old secret that had kindled an enthusiasm which was to carry us, without regret, through two years of toil and hardship to a climax so strange I can scarcely believe I did not dream it all.

Chapter II
UNDER WAY

THE train drew into Riobamba to lay over for the night before proceeding on up to Quito, Ecuador's capital. Here was the Hotel Metropolitano; and, waiting for us, Montford Hardwicke, a geologist; my nephew Alasdair Loch, fresh from a mining job in the Federated Malay States; and Peter Prime, a young student of botany from Wisconsin, another listener to the Expedition's broadcast over the A.R.R.L.

The next morning Carl and I went on to Quito to arrange with the government for permits to enter the Oriente territory, and to perform the other rituals that must be gone through with.

Quito meant a round of delightful dinners, newspaper interviews without end, and innumerable conferences with politicos in the various departments of government. The way was paved largely through letters brought down from the States; moreover, in many cases where there were no letters, kind friends in the foreign colony were ever ready to lend their aid.

Then back again to Riobamba, official matters over—at least I thought so. Then ensued a rechecking and sorting of equipment, an endless job that must be done, yet is never done.

Tents, ten flies; an outboard motor, tinned gasoline, camp cots for the lower regions; sleeping bags and blankets for the upper; mosquito nets, field boots, photographic and scientific equipment, rough field clothing, cooking utensils, dehydrated vegetables, meat extracts, rifles, carbines and pistols (George Brun, our hunter, saw to these with loving eye), medicinal supplies—a puzzle seemingly without solution. Much was to be left behind, for on the first phase of the Expedition my party was to be occupied only with the rivers of the lowlands.

We had been in Riobamba but a short time when an Indian bellboy came up to my room with word that I was wanted in the lobby on urgent business by a Señor Hector Moran. Grimy with dirt, hammer in hand amidst stacks of packing cases, I did not respond immediately. Soon the boy was back in an agitated state with word that Señor Moran was growing impatient.

"Sounds like a government official," Griswold said. "You'd better hurry."

Appreciating the possible importance of such a personage, I commenced to get agitated myself. What could he want with me? I thought it prudent, moreover, to wash, shave, change my shirt, and generally brush up in appearance.

I reached the lobby. There was no one there except a negro boy in a corner to one side. I turned towards the verandah; but, before I could leave, the bellboy crossed to the coal-black youth and paused at a respectful distance, seemingly too awed to speak.

The young negro was some fifteen years of age. He was dressed in a coat of brilliant, if faded, blue, and baggy, violently yellow trousers from which protruded, in spite of a languid undersized body, the most enormous feet I'd ever seen. Of shoes he had none—I wasn't surprised. And he was hatless, his shining woolly mop of hair topping off the lot.

Ignoring the bellboy with fine contempt, he stepped forward, bowed before me, then fixed me with an intent gaze.

"You are," he asked, "the 'Capitan'—the grand explorer?"

"I am Captain Loch," I said.

"Ah, I have read the papers. I am greatly interest—"

He broke off with a withering glare towards the bellboy who, after the manner of bellboys the world over, was quite obviously both waiting for a tip and eavesdropping on our conversation. No words were spoken. Not a sound issued from the thick lips, yet to my utter astonishment the bellboy, wilted, slunk away tipless to his corner.

"I am Señor Hector Moran!" He was a man of

action and went straight to the point—"I'm the best grand cook in Ecuador."

I thought I would have an apoplectic fit. The red surged up my neck as I thought up long-forgotten army oaths for having been so easily taken in.

Señor Hector Moran went on at a rapid rate. He had, he assured me, nerves of steel; his bravery knew no bounds. There was no wild animal, no savage Indian from Panama to Cape Horn with which he could not cope. Pressing letters of recommendation, suspiciously laudatory to have been come by honestly, into my unwilling hand, he drew a breath-taking picture of himself as a veritable dynamo of industry.

This was too much. Those indolent, lazy movements of his body were not to be belied. I cut the interview short. But the upshot was that Señor Hector Moran became cook, camp boy, and infallible source of aggravation to the Andes-Amazon Expedition from then on; he was taken on, not because he was a Stanley or Livingstone of a later day, nor because we needed a cook, but for a reason he would never have suspected.

In that brief wordless exchange with the Indian bellboy, I had seen that Hector Moran with his slick, city-trained mind, could get his own way with the Indians. Such a person, on occasions, could be an invaluable adjunct to any expedition.

Leaving Riobamba on September 11th we went by motor truck to the Hacienda Leito, some thirty-five miles east, a large, imposing house said to have been built a century or more before by the Jesuits. The present owner is one Restrepo, a Colombian, who welcomed us with the open hospitality of those parts.

Leito is a famous and historical hacienda mentioned (as Leytillo) in the old Guzman map. In fact it was here that the German scientist Guzman, one of the great students of the Llanganatis area, is said to have walked off the balcony in his sleep and been killed.

That the reader may form a better picture of Ecuador, I wish to point out that the Andes Mountains, here divided into two main ranges running north and south with lofty tablelands in between, literally split the country into three parallel sections or divisions.

Starting from the Pacific Ocean on the west, one first crosses the low-lying coastal zone or division and the *first* of the two mountain ranges, to reach the high tablelands, which lie at an altitude of from 7,000 to 9,000 feet or more. Although on the Equator, these picturesque, fertile lands, enclosed in a veritable corridor of peaks and volcanoes rising skyward to a height of 23,000 feet, are in a climate of perpetual springtime, and constitute the main settled and civilized zone of Ecuador.

To the east, across the second range of mountains, of which the Llanganatis form a part, isolating it from these civilized zones, lies the third and largest division of the country at the head of the upper Amazon Valley—the "Oriente." This is a little-known territory of low-lying torrid jungles peopled by divers tribes of Indians, through which flow the Curaray and Napo Rivers eastward to the Peruvian frontier. It is not generally known that this frontier encircles Ecuador not only on the south but on the east also, enfolding it, as it were, to the point where it joins Ecuador's northern neighbor, Colombia.*

The natural resources of the country are little developed, largely on account of the great difficulties of transportation and the geographical and topographical obstacles to be contended with. This is especially so in the case of the far-flung Oriente, whose isolation from the civilized centers is caused by the great barrier of the Llanganatis and adjacent groups. Existing trails make long detours, one to the north, the others to the south.

From a geographical standpoint our object was to search for a shorter line of air, land, and water communication from the western and central civilized zones over the Llanganatis Mountains and down the Curaray River to the far eastern Peruvian-Ecuadorian frontier and to map the uncharted region traversed. This purpose governed the whole itinerary determined upon by the Expedition. To reach the headwaters of this river and also to find an airplane landing field there was my first goal. (The journey was to be made by the circuitous trail which circumvents the Llanganatis by a long detour to the south.)

---

* From here on when allusion is made to the "frontier" or "Peruvian frontier" it refers only to that *eastern* part of the boundary where Peru adjoins Ecuador, and through which both the Curaray and Napo Rivers flow.

Consequently, here at Leito I prepared my party with equipment and supplies for the miles of tropical jungles that were ahead of us, while Carl de Muralt organized his group for a preliminary trip into the mountains.

Two more members were here added to the Expedition, Castillo, a Colombian, who joined us as an interpreter of Indian languages for the Oriente, and Napo, a dog of Great Dane heritage with a good many additions thereto and subtractions therefrom.

The hospitality of the Hacienda Leito was truly appreciated by all of us, for our long stay and the disturbing commotion of our preparations must have imposed considerably upon our host, Señor Marco Restrepo.

He is a vigorous man whose powers of work are infinite. Through this he has built up the hacienda to be one of the most successful in that part of the mountains. Everyone in the neighborhood is most justifiably scared to death of him, for he invariably carries a revolver with which he instantly despatches any of the innumerable dogs, cats, pigeons, mules, or other livestock that through some stupid act interfere with the hacienda's progress.

Our days here were full and busy ones which were an excellent break-in for all of us for our particular jobs. Hardwicke and Ohman were already hard at work testing and checking the instruments. Sonny Griswold fitted into the life with that rare adjustability to circumstances which is most truthfully his.

Equally at home whether leaning nonchalantly against the Ritz bar in New York, losing his money on horse-racing, or seated on a packing case outside a hut surrounded by a group of admiring Indian men, women, and children, plus the usual parrots and monkeys, he has dodged work in an office for the last thirty years with a skill of which his closer relatives are lamentably unappreciative.

George Brun, on the other hand, is a stern man. He seldom cracks a smile—save on such rare occasions as when a transport train, manipulated in some manner of which he may not happen to approve, misses its footing, and mules, loads, men, and rocks go hurtling down a hillside with the clatter of a dismembered locomotive. Whenever eventualities of this sort happen to *him* he invariably resorts to his most used expression, "What the *hell!*"

I was soon to hear him use it with great emphasis, for George Brun and Hector just couldn't get on.

It is true that as a special favor and with a certain amount of luck, Hector *could* be relied upon to boil water because he'd leave it on the fire and forget it, but beyond that, as a cook, well—the less said the better. I sympathized acutely with George, who, being in charge of supplies, naturally had direct control of Hector in the kitchen—a domain in which George happened to be unusually able. After a few days of exasperation with Hector, in desperation George was driven to take over that work himself. All went well, but there were some things that Hector hadn't seen before, and one of those was the particular brand of dried or desiccated fruits and vegetables which we had.

Opening a tin of what he deemed to be prunes, he passed a handful of the black granulated particles to George, who, without looking at them in the dim light of the kitchen, threw them into a pan which with a clatter he thrust onto the stove. It was at that moment I entered the kitchen to see what was going on.

I was greeted with a cloud of smoke as something shot past me. It was Hector—moving faster than he'd ever moved in his life and behind him a speechless, infuriated George, black from head to foot, gasping out, "Gun powder! What the *hell!*"

After this the diplomacy required to prevent the tiff between George and Hector from becoming a breach of such proportions that it might disrupt the whole Expedition at the outset would have taxed the skill of a European statesman.

Finally, both Carl's party and mine were ready: he, with Hardwicke and Alasdair, for the mountains; and I, with Griswold, George Brun, John Ohman, and Prime, for the distant Curaray. The day of parting came, and it was one that filled me with regret. Carl's support in the early stages of organizing the Expedition had been invaluable. In fact without him it might possibly not have materialized. We had anticipated months of intimate, eager work together, but as so often happens in the field, that was not to be. I was never to see him again until the Expedition was ended.

As I bade Carl good-by, I reflected on the sudden manner of our meeting and on how a small incident, maybe years before and of no significance at the time, can so influence our lives years later. A complete stranger to me at the outset of the Expedition, he was probably the one man besides myself out of New York's millions who was as enthusiastic as I about the Llanganatis Mountains. I realized with passing wonder that I might never have known Carl, and this Expedition never have come to pass, had I not, just twenty years before, lost my way, stumbled into a wrong camp and met a young man named Barclay.

It seems a far cry from the snowy peaks of Ecuador in 1935 to the World War and the Cameroon Campaign in West Africa in 1915; yet in a sense the story of this Expedition started there.

I was a young British subaltern of twenty-three at the time. Having been slightly wounded in the head, in danger of losing my eyesight, I was ordered back for medical treatment; while our column pushed farther into the Cameroons to attack the German settlement of Bamenda.

Chafing at being left behind, and my eyesight having improved, I determined to make a desperate attempt to rejoin the column, now well on ahead. The nature of the country between us and Bamenda, which was reported to be very difficult and had never been crossed by white men, had caused the column to take a long detour to the north. My only chance of catching up was to take a short cut across this intervening territory. Guided by my native orderly, who assured me he could accomplish this feat, we set off.

After many days we finally arrived in the vicinity of the column and were, we estimated, some day and a half's travel from our front line. But "front line" in that jungle-covered land hardly deserved such a flattering name. It consisted of nothing more than a series of what we called "perimeter" camps indiscriminately dotted about, where the men slept in a circle within close reach of one another in case of attack. No lights were permitted because of enemy snipers, and it would be an easy matter in the darkness to wander in between these camps right through to the enemy's lines. It was to one of these front-line perimeter camps that I had been ordered. Though it was far, I hoped by starting early to get through in one day.

I had miscalculated the difficulties ahead, however, and before I knew it was faced with the predicament of being overtaken by darkness in a district where one was just as liable to be shot down by one's own countrymen as by the enemy—if the sentries should be "jumpy" or should fail to recognize one in time.

To proceed was foolish, and my orderly and I were preparing to camp for the night as best we could when an unexpected sound, quite close at hand, struck my ears. It was a popular American ragtime song—and sung, much to my relief, in English!

Pushing carefully through the bush I saw, as the jungle thinned, a camp on a lone knoll brightly illuminated by the ruddy glare of a blazing campfire, around which were seated a group of officers. It wasn't my camp, nor my affair, but it certainly seemed a pleasant place to spend the night.

No longer concerned about having to camp in the jungle, I pushed my way into the group. In the center a young Englishman was seated on an upturned packing case, singing the latest song hits from America. His name was Barclay, and we hit it off at once.

Little did I dream at that time what an important part in my life this meeting was to play twenty years later.

Our friendship was fated to be of short duration, for soon afterwards he was killed in the course of the Campaign. But during our acquaintance he had frequently mentioned a cousin of his, John Barclay, then in the Intelligence at the War Office in London, whom I met later, at the close of the Campaign, at a London party.

John Barclay and I became friends, but during those hectic days that followed we lost track of each other. The War ended, the years passed, and I came to America—to have my dreams of going to the Llanganatis.

Leaving the Public Library that fateful day in the Spring of '35, I bumped right square into my old friend again! Almost before he could speak, I fairly shouted at him—"I'm going to the Llanganatis Mountains to find the—"

He laughed aloud, but his laugh was suddenly cut short. "The Llanganatis!" he said, "that's strange. Why, I know a man who—"

He introduced me to Bill Klamroth, who, knowing of my plans, immediately introduced me to his friend Carl de Muralt! And at this meeting was formed the Andes-Amazon Expedition, in whose destiny we were all to have our share.

Chapter III
FAREWELL TO CIVILIZATION

Two days on muleback over an easy trail eastwards down the valley of the Rio Pastaza brought us to Puyo at an elevation of some 3,000 feet.

Puyo is a small town on the fringe of the Oriente and is the jumping-off place for the deep interior. It is the end of the mule trail, and from here on we were to proceed with Indian carriers.

Again followed the endless exertion, in a now tropical and enervating heat, of splitting the equipment into smaller loads, for each carrier was to shoulder seventy-five pounds—no more, no less.

Previously I had sent on ahead to arrange for the Indians. Of recent years, however, a great shortage of these had developed here, compelling us at times to use women and to carry on much of our freighting from here to the Curaray in shifts.

Here at Puyo I was to meet a famous character, Severo Vargas. An Indian "Chief"—or rather overlord—I had heard of him before. Half Canelo and half Jivaro Indian, he was immensely proud of the fierce untamed blood he had acquired from the latter. Thickset, powerful, and sharp-eyed, at some time in his life he had been shot through the face, the bullet entering beside his nose and coming out at the back of his neck. The resultant wound had somewhat depleted his energies, but he was still a great power in the district.

Through the evenings Vargas would stand vigorously declaiming to me the story of his life.

Some sixty years before, his father, a Canelo Indian, had married his mother, a member of the neighboring Jivaros. This "love match," of which Vargas was the result, had brought to these two ever warring tribes a lasting and enduring peace. The two tribes, both strengthened by this union, now made war on the Arapicos, another group; and Vargas' youth was a merry one of fighting, head-shrinking, and other such horseplay.

But clouds arose on the horizon, first priests, then policemen. They would have no more of Vargas and his playful tribal ways, and the old man shook his head with sorrow as he told of the great change Law and Order had effected.

But Vargas was no fool, and, being unusually ambitious for an Indian, had thrown himself into an energetic pursuit of the ways of the white man. The result was disastrous, for long before I met him he had decided that civilization meant trickery, fraud, deception, and all conceivable forms of imposture and chicanery.

Into these new fields he had launched himself with an enthusiasm that was highly commendable. He soon had made of himself a master craftsman in those arts, looking upon them as a legitimate form of buffoonery. He carried out his chicanery with a boisterous good humor that was quite captivating.

He was truly a grand old ruffian, and, if he liked you, would do a lot for you.

Trouble commenced at once. It turned out that our contractor for transportation from Leito to the Curaray, a negro, had once been a policeman! (How can an expedition's leader know *everything?*)

Now Vargas' pet aversions were priests and policemen; and, of course, such prejudices cannot be overcome in a day. What Vargas did I never really knew, but as time went on our contractor commenced to wear a puzzled, worried look. He grew restless, irritable, and depressed. The upshot of it all was that the wages asked of him by the Indian carriers suddenly jumped sky high. That brought me into the picture with martial stride. The contractor's failure to get Indians at a reasonable price was holding up our progress. I tackled old Vargas. I knew it was his doing.

"How can he pay such prices?" I demanded. "He's contracted with me at a certain figure!"

"But a policeman!"

"He will be ruined, I shall be ruined, the Expedition—the United States will be ruined!"

"But a *policeman!*" he deprecated with outstretched hands.

I was quite firm, and he promised to do nothing further to hinder our progress. But, promises or not, before dawn the next morning the contractor had fled precipitately—contract scattered to the winds—back to his home, wife, and child, which he decided needed protection from the vengeance of Severo Vargas, who forthwith became major-domo of the Expedition.

On October 4th we moved down the Rio Puyo by canoe to Indyllama. Another day by foot and we were in Canelos on the Rio Bobonaza, a tributary of the Pastaza. Then eastward, ever eastward, down the Bobonaza for a day to an Indian house called "Chambira," which had been established for the use of anyone moving along the river. Two more days of difficult walking, sometimes laborious climbing, over a narrow trail, muddy with the rains of weeks and slippery to the point of being dangerous, through dense tangled vegetation of the forest-covered slopes of the mountains which enfolded us on all sides, and we were in Huito, on the Rio Villano, the last outpost of civilization this side of the distant frontier.

All this sounds simple in the extreme; yet actually it was nothing of the sort. On the map the terrain covered seems a bagatelle, but in jungle travel the shortest route between two points is seldom if ever a straight-line distance between the two. I question that, save for the river phase, our course ever went one hundred yards in a direct line. The solid walls of lush, rich jungle made a barrier almost impossible to penetrate, for within a yard or so of the beaten path one became enmeshed in a tangled, sinuous web—a world apart. The Indians had discovered long before our advent that the wise man reaches his objective in the jungle, not necessarily by forcing his trail in a straight line, but often by a circuitous route of least resistance which conserves his strength and temper.

We suffered the usual expected delays—carriers slithering and toppling, equipment falling into the bush and having to be rescued. Rest periods also took their toll, and chance meetings with other Indians on the trail resulted in those inevitable social amenities so much beloved by Indians, which might have lasted hours each time had I not been there to forestall them.

Old Vargas was the one who always got them started again; yet once the effort was made and they were getting on the move, it was Hector Moran who would stand ostentatiously in a place where I could not help but see him, get in everybody's way, and shout, "Vamos! Vamos! Vamos!" and turn to me with a self-satisfied look as if he were the real driving force behind the Expedition.

Vargas was quite a problem to him. He watched the old man closely and appeared to be fretting constantly over some secret sorrow. I called him sharply aside.

"Hector—Hector Moran! You can't put it over on him. He's a great man."

Hector's decision was instantaneous.

"So? Then I will become his friend."

Huito was a little cluster of Indian houses with its mission. It was presided over by a "traveling bishop," Padre Leon. I found him a remarkable old man, fanatical about his missionary work, which had expanded constantly over the last sixty years, and holding a tremendous influence over the Indians by reason of his ministrations to them.

I was much impressed by the astonishing punctuality with which he got them to attend his Sunday services. At the first bell canoes would put out from across the river, and from all parts of the small colony Indian men, women, and children would collect outside the mission. A second bell, and one and all would enter, the doors closing immediately behind them.

There were no belated stragglers, no last-minute arrivals seeking admission.

This was all the more remarkable when one considers that, to Indians, to lay stress on such a thing as punctuality is just another proof of the white man's foolish ways. The Indian knows dawn and sunset, tomorrow and the next "moon," and that is all that concerns him.

Padre Leon generously turned over to us the use of his house, but, in answer to my request for Indians to accompany us, appeared quite dubious.

Already I was beginning to hear talk of the

"Aucas." The name "Aucas," meaning wild or savage people, is locally applied to the Ssabela Indians, a hostile tribe living between the Curaray and the Napo Rivers.

"A year or two ago," Padre Leon said, "a war party of them even reached the outskirts of Huito itself, killing several of the inhabitants."

At the time I rather doubted this party was composed of Aucas; yet it was true that a few weeks before our arrival a small band of them had murdered a man and a woman several miles away.

The effect on the Expedition was instantaneous. Our Indian cook, engaged to replace Hector's aimless meanderings in the kitchen, deserted on the spot and vanished into the bush.

For the "Aucas" to come so far from their own hunting grounds, right through the Zaparo territory, seemed to me indeed unusual. I could not understand it.

I was considerably set back by the Padre's information, for the Rio Villano (meaning "villain") flows into the Curaray; and it was by going down this tributary that we hoped to reach that great river, there to obtain the aid of the friendly Zaparos. From them we had great expectations of obtaining a fine collection of ethnological specimens and data for the Museum, and upon their aid we depended for the descent and mapping of the Curaray to the frontier.

The whole region between Huito and Puyo is sadly depopulated today. Smallpox, fevers, and a type of influenza have all taken their toll through the "super-stitions of the elders," according to Vargas. Presumably, he meant lack of sanitation and ignorance of modern medical science; for even he certainly could not have meant the priests, who are wonderfully good to Indians in administering every medical attention possible. The Church has had a great influence on the Indian life of these regions.

Time went by in Huito pleasantly enough, and we had our diversions, chief among them being a wedding on the grand scale.

The bride was a resident of the settlement; and the groom had come from somewhere nearby, accompanied by various and innumerable aunts, uncles, cousins, friends, dogs, and more personal animal life.

The good Padre extended to us an invitation to attend the ceremony which, of course, was to include a lengthy church service. This latter was too much for the Expedition, which disappeared to a man into the bush—all except Griswold who, unsuspectingly, was watching some Indian girls bathing in the river through our theodolite telescope.

"Come to church," I said sternly. I knew that I was stuck, and I refused to suffer alone.

He stared at me aghast. "But I haven't been to church for twenty years."

"Nor have I." Nevertheless I was adamant.

Our altercation made us late, and we sheepishly eased our way amidst the throng in a futile attempt to avoid the Padre's searching glance.

Soon we were well on into the wedding ceremony. Suddenly a terrific "boom" reverberated across the river and echoed back from the surrounding hills.

Damn! George Brun! Of course! To avoid going to church he had decided to go fishing in the pool below the mission.

Fishing in those parts not being a sport for pleasure, but only an earnest search for that all-important thing, food, George had taken with him the customary stick of dynamite with which to kill the fish. Now he had his reward—at least so he thought.

But at the first detonation the bridegroom, accompanied by the aforesaid various and innumerable aunts, uncles, cousins, friends, and dogs, knowing the significance of the explosion, burst from the ceremony with wild yells of glee, tore off their clothing, and a moment later, to George's utter disgust, were deep in the river retrieving for themselves such fish as had been killed.

Not satisfied with this, no sooner were the fish caught, than the whole party went off to their huts to devour the catch, leaving a solitary little bride to whimper all by herself.

Whether the wedding was ever completed, I shall never know. Maybe, in true Indian fashion, they let the whole matter slide.

I was careful to avoid the good Padre's eye that night.

Wooing a girl, with some of these tribes, was once, and, I believe, sometimes still is, a merry little prank that has been played very seriously for many centuries.

The whole onus of the matter, the outcome of which is usually clearly understood at the outset, falls upon the two fathers of the prospective couple, who, being very young themselves, may understand nothing of what is happening.

The father of the boy, selecting two friends to support him throughout his arduous ordeal, proceeds to the house of the girl's father, armed with large quantities of chicha (native beer). This is done suddenly or by stealth; for, upon seeing them approach, the girl's father may fly helter-skelter from his house —to avoid being asked the auspicious question, which in any case it is the code for him to refuse at the first asking. His flight can be arrested and violently obstructed by the others. If the girl herself happens to be present, she will always be permitted to escape into the jungle, where she remains until the whole business is over.

Once successfully cornered, the girl's father will now be appealed to by the applicant, who, throwing himself down in a position of complete submission, will perform an age-old ritual, which begins with a long-winded succession of ejaculations, of which the following are only a few:

> For your hearthstones!
> For the supporting posts of your house!
> For the flesh of your body!
> For your yuca!

For your blood!
If you hit me!
If you hit me with your hands!
If you hit me with a stick!
If you kill me and throw my dead body away!

Meanwhile the girl's father has the right to slap and kick the supplicant, throwing the proffered chicha in his face, to which the latter replies by extolling the virtues of his son, although he is permitted the relaxation of a little private blasphemy of his own directed towards his two supporting henchmen, who add words of sympathy for his dire position.

These violent tactics on the part of the girl's father are usually pursued only when he intends the marriage ultimately to take place, for should he do this and still refuse the girl, it is one of the few insults and personal affronts that will be remembered for a long time. This may even lead to the employment of witchcraft on the part of the insulted man and his friends, or, at the least, a fight at the next drunken party.

The first attempt is always a fruitless one, and these sportive antics have to be gone all over again and again—depending no doubt on the quantity of chicha that happens to be easily obtainable.

Here chicha is made from yuca, the South American tuber somewhat like the yam; and, if the process of manufacturing is not pleasant to contemplate, the finished produce is certainly most efficacious, for it leaves the Indians who drink it too inebriated to care whether school keeps or not.

The yuca is masticated at great length by the women of the tribe, whose facial contortions during this procedure are wonderful to behold. The residue is then spit into a bowl; and the sickly stuff, after several days of fermentation, becomes alcoholic.

Chicha is always made by the women, for the reason that yuca—at least in the case of the Jivaro head-shrinkers dwelling farther south—has a female soul. This "soul business" offers great opportunities in the Jivaro country, where a very pleasant social system has been worked out. It seems that every product or activity upon which their lives depend is given either a male or a female soul, the custom being that only men may handle things which pertain to the male soul, while the women's work is confined to those things relating to the female soul.

But it must have been a man who thought of this, for all the light or pleasant work, such as hunting and the like, appears to have a male soul; whereas the heavy duties—such as tilling the soil, making pottery and cooking utensils, even carrying the heavy burdens on the trail—well, all these things have *female* souls; so, of course, the men mustn't touch them.

Maybe Severo Vargas, himself half Jivaro, had something to do with this.

A few days after our arrival Padre Leon left the tiny settlement for Canelos, a picturesque figure in rusty, tucked-up cassock, slouch hat, and high field boots. A rosary suspended around his neck rested beneath his long beard.

After his departure we discovered in his bedroom a bamboo stabbing sword or dagger, the point dipped in the deadly curare poison. What origin or purpose it might have I never learned, but it struck me as a strange weapon for the old man to possess.

My thoughts followed the kindly Padre, and I marveled at how the missionaries get about in such inaccessible places. They carry little or no baggage and live among Indian tribes that have only ceased being hostile in the last few decades. Such mobility always brings a feeling of envy to those on a cumbersome expedition; for cumbersome we were, but unavoidably so. We were a large party for such a trip, which meant a large amount of baggage. But as it turned out, I was very glad we had these supplies with us.

Even the Padre's influence could not readily secure us canoes or Indians to take us to the Curaray, and there followed days of haggling with the curaca, or headman, of the Huito Indians. He could get no one to leave Huito on such a "terrible" trip as we planned. In fact we came to a point where he suggested that it would be safer for the longevity of all concerned if I went back to Puyo, to Quito—caramba!—to my native Scotland.

However, an abrupt change occurred overnight, an inexplicable transformation. Eight stalwart Indians suddenly declared their great happiness would be to smooth our path ahead. They would go to the

Curaray, to the border, or to hell if we so desired. They would do anything we wished. They——

Such a sudden change of feeling deserved investigation.

It appeared that during one of our regular radio schedules someone connected with the Expedition had absented himself and strolled to the curaca's house. His mission was to pass on a great secret for the curaca's benefit. The secret was that in talking with El Presidente in Quito I was said to have told him of the wonders of Huito and that we liked the town so much we were even planning to live in it a year or more, maybe forever.

Instantly the curaca became a man of action. "A year or more." This was too much for him; his hitherto quiet life had already been badly disrupted by our arrival and the fact that Padre Leon frequently made him work for us. Our pestilential presence could now only be corrected by our departure. The sooner we started the better, and overnight we had our men.

Whose was the genius, the mastermind, that thought up this beautifully faked radio conversation? John Ohman was beyond reproach. He would not lie even for the Expedition. Severo Vargas? No, that was too subtle for him.

I turned, and there before me, looking disdainfully out over the river, was Señor Hector Moran! I sought no farther.

Chapter IV
THE CURARAY AT LAST

On October 4th we put off down the Rio Villano, glad to be on our way.

It was a picturesque leave-taking, John Ohman and I in the first canoe with three paddlers, the others strung out behind in a long line.

Now work for us began in earnest, for we were anxious to provide the American Geographical Society and the Royal Geographical Society with complete data on this hitherto sketchily mapped area. We took bearings in rapid succession, "shot" the sun frequently, and sketched every bend and straightaway in the twisting, tortuous stream. Scientific records had to be carefully kept, there was always equipment to worry about, and the thousand and one smaller jobs which make exploring anything but the pleasant, easy life it is pictured, were always omnipresent.

Meanwhile we rounded turns or shot over riffles to the discomfort of innumerable parrots and parrakeets; chattering monkeys fled at our approach, standing off at a distance and screaming at us end-lessly.

It was a country already rich in such bigger game as jaguars, tapirs, ocelots, and the like; but, unless one is out to hunt them, it is surprising how few can be seen.

No little time was lost in retrieving the dog Napo, who needed but a movement in the brush to be over the side and away, splashing water over everyone in the immediate vicinity. Whether ashore or afloat we carried on a constant war against the myriad flies, gnats, and mosquitoes that defied tobacco smoke, or anything else. Shoals had to be waded, and once we were forced to stop before a large tree which had fallen across the river and through which we literally had to chop a passage.

It was a far cry from anything we had seen here-tofore, a plunging, racing stream one moment and a sluggish, brackish backwater the next, eerie in its solitude and vaguely awe-inspiring in the immensity of the surrounding territory.

Not a living person did we see nor any evidences of humans; yet I felt sure that this was true only of the Rio Villano. Farther down on the Curaray we would find Zaparos aplenty, according to what I had been told in New York and Ecuador.

It was around midday that a remarkable thing happened which, had I not seen it with my own eyes, I would have found hard to believe. A short distance ahead was a slender green snake swimming leisurely across the river from one bank to another. As we drew nearer, he headed straight across our path, having no intention of abandoning the even tenor of his way; nor would the flow of the river allow us to stop.

As luck would have it, he barged right into the side of our moving canoe. Thinking no doubt that we were just another log floating down river, he was out of the water with a single flip of his tail, across our outriding balsa log, over the side, and into the bottom of the canoe. He wiggled about a moment, passed over John's legs, then took off over the opposite side into the water and was back on his course.

The snake was an "utsukulin," said by the Indians to be very poisonous. Luck was with John that day. He was well out of the encounter.

Then again the monotony of solid jungle walls hemming us in, bearings to be taken with the Brunton compass, the sun to be shot ever and again, the chronometer to be worried over for fear it had lost or gained a few seconds since our last check by radio with Washington, the incessant diaries to be kept, sketching, slapping flies, stopping laboriously to wade a hundred yards past a shoal, the confusion of a canoe tilting and half filling, wetting records painfully acquired and frequently spoiling foodstuffs.

The fear that had come to me farther back on seeing no Indians en route arose to plague me again when we reached a settlement called Muriti, which the curaca at Huito had said was a village. The village proved to be a single hut, deserted and with no signs of recent occupancy.

We spent the night on a sand bar by the river, and a weird night it was. A campfire blazing fitfully in the abysmal murk, moths flitting by ghoulishly, and creatures of all kinds resenting our intrusion into their domain. It was a brilliant moonlight night, and we lay awake wondering what the future would hold. Would the Curaray River prove the navigable waterway to the frontier which we hoped for?

The second day was largely a repetition of the first, though the river widened at the junction of the Rio Lliquino, where we were told we would find an Indian settlement; but, as before, we found nothing.

It was while descending the Villano, sitting back in the canoe and listening to the Indians' accounts of the Aucas, that I first heard the story of "the white chief with a beard." Tall and light of skin, he was believed to have given the Aucas a highly organized and quite complex social system.

If it is true that there is or was a "white chief" somewhere in the heart of the Ssabelas' territory, the most plausible theory to account for such a thing would be that of a renegade white man. Who could he be, I wondered!

I had heard of a certain foreigner who went native on the Arajuno River and whose daughter was reputed to have come down from New York to prevail on him to return to civilization. Shortly afterwards the father disappeared and later was reported to be living far to the south with another tribe.

Ever since leaving Huito we had seen no sign of human life whatever. The river appeared deserted in spite of all I had been led to expect.

Early in the afternoon of our fifth day the Indians showed their first overt fear of this silent country. We had been going down the river as usual, when I was suddenly brought up short by the lurch of the canoe as it wheeled round and nosed into a sandbank. Glancing up, I saw the Indians frozen rigid, pointing at a spot in the sand and saying far more through looks and gestures than words could have conveyed. Paying no attention to me, they were out of the canoe in a twinkling and standing over a lone footprint. One or two went a short distance into the bush, but returned hurriedly.

The unquestionably genuine fright of the Indians at this strange footprint was manifested by their furious activity with the paddles when we regained our canoe. Previously, I had begun to fear that we would not reach the Curaray that night, as we had intended. But there was no doubt now. There was to be no camp for them on any strange sandbank that night.

With John assisting at the paddles we made good time; and, as darkness fell, we turned the bend, and through an opening in the trees beheld that great broad river which had been so constantly in my thoughts for months—the Curaray River.

It was now quite dark, but a few turns down the river we found a tiny cluster of Indian huts.

The place rejoiced in the name of Puerto Tunghurahua, and was presided over by a solitary white man, José Vicuna.

Great was the excitement of the small group of Indians who flocked to meet us when they learned that we intended to get into the Auca country after descending the Curaray. To do so, they declared, was to court certain death.

Seated around the fire that night, our every move watched by the meager band of friendly Indians that hemmed us in, I looked across at Vicuna and broached the subject uppermost in my mind.

"We must have men!"

"There are none here," said Vicuna. "It is the Land of Nadie-Nadie,"—then almost to himself, "Nadie-Nadie."

"The 'Land of No One-No One'? Where are the Zaparos?"

He shrugged and spread his hands in a gesture of hopelessness. "There are none left!"

Chapter V
"HOW CAN THE CHILDREN LIVE—"

Thıs dearth of men was desperate news, and my hopes of collecting ethnological specimens for the Museum vanished on the instant.

In addition, all our plans for the descent of the Curaray had to undergo a change. No longer could we rely upon friendly Indians for canoes and supplies. Rafts, which can be handled by fewer men, would have to be built to reach the frontier. But these, of course, could not be used to travel back against the current. Our return then up the Curaray would be impossible. An arduous journey north to the Napo, thence up that river in canoe, would be the only way.

But worse than either of these, the disappearance of the Zaparos precluded all possibility of that "friendly" introduction to the Aucas which we so badly needed, and which is the only intelligent approach to such a hostile, independent people.

My original intention had been to enter the wild

territory of the Ssabela tribe from the south—that is, from the Curaray side. But I was now forced to postpone our entry into Rayo Urcu, the flat mesa at the west end of the area, until we had concluded our trip to the Peruvian frontier, then to approach it from the north, while en route up the Napo River, which was now our last recourse for obtaining sufficient Indians for such an undertaking.

"Rayo Urcu," Vicuna interrupted me, "is a very bad place. The Aucas there are more hostile than anywhere."

I understood what he meant when I recalled a current story that the Auca tribe had split, the western group going to Rayo Urcu to live in a "town on a precipice beside a waterfall."

It was quite true that most Auca outrages of recent years of which I could obtain any sound evidence appeared to have been perpetrated by them from this Rayo Urcu; and it was from there that the attack on the Hacienda Capricio on the Curaray had been launched a year and nine months previously. One of the few to escape was a cripple, Padilla, who hid in a hollow tree and witnessed the whole affair and told me the story himself.

Shortly after, the hacienda, the last one on the Curaray, was abandoned, the little group of survivors fleeing down river to found a new settlement which they called Puerto Tunghurahua, where I now met them.

The owner of Capricio, one Carlos Sevilla, had been a victim of another assault some years before.

Coming up the Nuschino en route to Napo with a crew of Zaparo paddlers, he had reached a narrow point in the river called Yana Rumi when the blow fell.

An avalanche of spears shot out from the overhanging bank. Instantly all the Indians with him jumped overboard. The sudden shift threw him after them before he could seize his carbine. Eventually, thrusting his head up, he saw the Aucas completing their murderous work. Managing to reach shore, he plunged into the jungle; and at a clearing some distance from the river he met one of his paddlers who had been speared while running up the bank. Though the weapon still protruded through his abdomen, the man cried, "Patron, pull the spear from my belly and let us follow the savages to avenge our people."

Sevilla eased his suffering as best he could; but they had gone only a few hundred yards when the Zaparo fell dead. Almost immediately Sevilla was captured and taken to the river bank, where the Aucas found his hat and were delighted with it. During the excitement he plunged into the river, although badly wounded through the body, and made his escape. For eight days he wandered aimlessly, subsisting on what he could find, crossing swollen rivers and trackless forests, and at last reaching his home.

Among other survivors of attacks was a girl who had seen her father speared before her eyes and who had an even more brutal story of an uncle's death. Very excitedly she related the grim details. From her and others I gleaned more word of the Aucas' extreme hostility to people from the outside, and of the fate that had met Roggierone on his gold hunting expedition. And again, as so often in the past, the specter of the "white chief with a beard" was told with only slight changes.

Regretfully enough, all such tales have to be taken with a very large grain of salt, as do any Indian stories, for that matter, the first or second time of hearing. I had long since discovered that an Indian's account of an occurrence, if you are successful in getting one at all on your initial questioning, will vary greatly from what you will hear later. This may come from a variety of causes, not necessarily because of a deliberate intention to lie. The teller may be afraid of you, afraid to tell you anything; then again he will be very apt to give you the version that he thinks will please you most.

Add to this a myriad of ulterior motives of his own, and it can be well understood how extremely difficult it is to obtain accurate information even from eyewitnesses of events. Great care must be used in questioning to give no impression of anxiety, lest the answer will be what he thinks you wish it to be.

The best way to get round the situation is to collect all the stories your informant offers you from time to time and strike an average.

So the "white chief with a beard" caused me no

concern; yet in checking back over my notes I find that I met this same apparition, with varied modifications, at a dozen points passed by the Expedition. More strangely, it appeared in places far distant from each other. There was even one Auca woman, who had supposedly been captured from the tribe as a child during this mysterious personage's reign. It was a point worthy of mention, however, that she admitted she had never seen him.

At the same time she did remember; in fact, she was very sure of it, having seen other Auca chiefs, or sub-chiefs, with beards, a strange anomaly, since Indians in these regions are rarely able to grow hair on their faces unless there has been some infusion of white blood, such as in the case of the Jivaros, after that historic attack on the large Spanish settlement of Sevilla del Oro, where, after the men had been killed, the white women were taken.

The complete disappearance of the Zaparos was indeed surprising. Only a few years before they had been a large and prosperous tribe, renowned for their relatively advanced state of civilization and famous for their pottery and especially for their knotless hammocks woven out of the fiber of the chambira palm. They were adepts, too, at the manufacture of the "wooden blankets and cloths" made, as many of the surrounding tribes do, out of the bark of the llanchama tree.

It is strange how Indian tribes, sometimes quite large as in the case of the Zaparos, can completely disappear in a relatively very short time. I recall hearing a story of a tribe, Crucitas I think was their name, that lived to the northwest on the Napo River some years ago.

There had been quite a number of them, and they dressed peculiarly in long smocks, of their own ingenious design, which extended down to their ankles.

They worked for no one but used to wash gold with which they would come into Napo Town to sell or barter. They were a friendly people and were well known in the district by their regular visits and unusual clothing.

Suddenly, as if by a prearranged signal, they ceased to come to Napo; and from that day onwards were never seen again.

Some little while afterwards a man went into their area prospecting and found nothing but ruined habitations grown over by the jungle. What the explanation of their disappearance was has never been discovered. Some scourge of sickness may have destroyed them or driven them away. But no trace of them has been found elsewhere.

Some say that they migrated to the higher paramos, for one large hacienda, extending for great distances to the east of the high, civilized tableland, commenced to have trouble with cattle stealing in the outlying confines of its property. The thieves were tracked, but never caught; but the trackers found signs of freshly killed meat still drying on a drying frame of a style used only in the Oriente and quite unlike that made by the mountain Indians.

Here in Puerto Tunghurahua I discovered a forlorn little band of three Zaparos, who, upon being questioned, brought more dismal stories of the diminution of their people. Fevers, scourges, and Aucas —always Aucas—had driven them from their homeland.

Aucas were the "worst people on earth"; and, as the eldest of the group left me, he summed up all their misfortunes in one pathetic, unanswerable sentence:

"How can the children live if the parents die?"

Little did he know that before I was to leave Ecuador he and another of the trio were to join their vanished tribesmen at the points of Auca spears.

The whole turn of events upset Severo Vargas, who now saw additional work and trouble ahead. Either for this reason or because he saw an opportunity for a try at extra pay, he gave notice for himself and his men that they were leaving as soon as we reached the frontier post of Tarqui. To his astonishment I accepted without demur. He knew nothing of the change of plans to attempt to reach Rayo Urcu later with men from the Napo River, at which point, being out of his "territory," his services could be dispensed with.

Since canoes for the whole party were out of the question, we set about building large rafts made out of the buoyant balsa trees. Pinioned together with crosstrees, lashed with long strips of bark, with raised platforms over which we erected our tent flies for protection against the weather, these craft would be a pleasant change from the restricted dugout canoes.

Here we seemed far from the influence of civilized life, and it amused me to remember that many maps of Ecuador show a convenient railroad running right to the Curaray River! It was a promotion scheme of some years back, and like many such schemes came to nothing. The railroad was never built, but this did not inconvenience or discourage the cartographer, who blithely engraved it on one edition of a map of Ecuador which has since gone all over the world. Not long ago I received a letter from a man, a stranger to Ecuador, asking how many *minutes* it takes to reach the Curaray.

During this time we lived in a good-sized Indian hut which Vicuna made available to us. We were comfortable enough on the flat cane floor raised four to five feet above the ground.

Hector here reached new heights. Now it is not an easy matter to arouse by one single act the rage of five different men, each engaged upon completely diverse tasks, at one and the same moment. Yet Hector achieved this, for he carefully elected to light the midday cooking fire beneath our floor immediately under the spot where we were sitting. Instantly we were on our feet in paroxysms of coughing, choking, and sniffing. We cursed the fire, the cook, and all things that had brought about Hector's birth.

Incensed, I drove him away with an enormous pile

of Expedition laundry, which I knew would keep him busy for hours. Providing him with an ample bar of soap, I sternly set him a time limit on pain of dire penalty.

Returning to the house a short time later, I found him still sitting there, gazing dreamily into the remains of the fire. I waited.

When his time limit was up, I demanded our laundry, a dangerous smile on my face. Whereupon Hector led me to long rows of immaculate, snowy-white clothing drying on the nearby bushes. I was dumbfounded.

The explanation was not long in coming. Cornered, Hector haltingly admitted that, retaining half the bar of soap for his own personal use, he had bribed all the available Indian women with a gift of the remainder and then lolled back idly while, with breathless, sweating efforts on the banks of the river, the women washed our clothes by beating them on stones without the use of any soap whatever. Hector had gone into the laundry racket!

Our rafts were finally ready; but, before we could get off, the rain came on in torrents. It was a fortunate thing we hadn't started, as the rain continued without cessation for several days and nights, bringing the river down in a heavy flood impossible for either raft or canoe to negotiate. This forced us into long hours of inactivity in the congested space of the hut. We passed the time as best we could, I writing up the reports of the trip, the others with their several occupations, and John Ohman keeping us in touch with civilization by his invaluable radio and ever taking a thousand and one odd and unexpected jobs upon his willing shoulders.

Rain, damp heat, flies, and mud—we had them in abundance. It was enervating and dispiriting, and we began to get very tired of our cramped quarters, a sentiment which was not shared, however, by the insect life of the neighborhood, which seemed to flock to our abode in increasing numbers. Innumerable cockroaches which seemed as big as dinosaurs gamboled playfully over the floor, passing the time of day with centipedes the size of caterpillar tractors.

I remember a big bird-eating spider, locally known as a "machin" and boasting a proud six inches across his "leg spread," which appeared in the rafters above our heads and seemed to be at home in a mass of coarse web. This was a surprise, for I had been told these did not weave webs for the purpose of habitation. However, I understand that the male in the mating season weaves a small platform on which he spreads his fertilizing secretion. It is then drawn into two "feelers" by means of which he injects it into the female, after which he runs for his life to avoid the merry custom of the female, as a rule larger in size than her mate, to immediately chase and kill her lover.

Meanwhile the sun had become only a memory we had known far behind in civilization; the rain kept falling without a break from a sullen sky; and frequently from the jungle around us we heard the resounding crash of falling trees.

In fact it was a day of falls, for the steps to this house as to others of its type consisted of a round log with notches cut in one side, the whole set at an angle. To the barefooted natives this forms an easy stairway, but to a man with boots, in wet weather especially, it is a menace. I think in the course of our stay every member of the Expedition fell down it with a resounding thump, including Napo, the dog. Everything became so slippery from the moisture that on the day set for our departure even the Indians could not climb the palm trees to which we had attached our radio antenna. We recovered it at last by shooting it down—a process which, though successful, was most effective in lightening our ammunition supply.

Finally a break came in the weather, and the river receded. Eagerly we packed our belongings, and on our two rafts, augmented by the three small canoes we had obtained, at four o'clock in the afternoon we pushed out into the stream. The current soon caught us, and swept us steadily down the river—into the Land of Nadie-Nadie.

Above: Expedition in the Oriente
Left to right: (*Standing*) Bolivar Castillo (*interpreter*), George Brun, Severo Vargas; (*seated*) Peter Prime with Napo, John Ohman, Sonny Griswold, Hector Moran

Below: George Brun on a Balsa Raft on the Curaray River

The Only Ssabela Indian Ever Photographed

Chapter VI
THE LAND OF NADIE-NADIE

FOUR o'clock in the afternoon may seem an odd hour to embark for parts unknown, but raft travel carries with it few of the discomforts of moving by canoe. On reaching a favorable spot one merely paddles himself ashore, makes the raft fast, and relaxes. The fire is lit and the evening meal all ready. No unloading or repacking is necessary.

Raft travel is the most convenient way of moving down jungle rivers, as these craft are capable of sustaining great weights and can, if necessary, be handled by very few men. But woe betide you if you strike a sunken tree or rock; for let but one log break free and your raft soon disintegrates, dumping you and your precious baggage overboard. To be quite up to date at this time we named these rafts "Normandie" and "Queen Mary."

Again ensued the familiar charting, sketching, and sounding of the Curaray. Miles without end of solid jungle encompassed us on every side. We drifted past a riotous tangle of heavy undergrowth and hanging vines through which the heads of majestic palms would thrust themselves upward as if for air. There was the taraputu, a palm valued for its hard, durable wood used extensively by the Indians for supports to their huts and for spears and other weapons; and the chambira, famed for its "thread" fiber used for fish nets, hammocks, carrying bags, and the like. There were also kili, shiwa, ramus, and that never-to-be-forgotten slender little palm which, with bark of silvery white and graceful drooping blue-green leaves, is so aptly called in Quechua, *panigua*, meaning "little sister." We were devoured by the most voracious "moscos" (a small black biting fly) I have ever known; and the usual attentions followed from chigoes (jiggers), garapatas (ticks), biting gnats, fleas, flies, wasps, centipedes, ants, scorpions, and other annoying inhabitants of the jungle.

Vampire bats commenced to reach our rafts. These minute marauders—they are only two or three inches in length—are quite common in the South American tropics and cause considerable trouble with horses and cattle, but in the interior are apt to give their attention to humans and appear to prefer certain individuals over others. On finding one to their liking, they have been known to return to him night after night.

For several days previously we had noticed a change in the hitherto irrepressible Hector. He had become morose and low-spirited, and under questioning admitted he had been a victim. Even Napo had shown listlessness and grown thin to the point of emaciation.

On one occasion John and Prime reported having witnessed an interesting occurrence the previous night. Napo was sleeping at the foot of their cots when suddenly a vampire bat winged silently in, settled a few feet from him, and spent several moments in close scrutiny. Contrary to public belief, when the men turned on their flashlights the bat did not depart. It moved forward and crawled onto the dog's paw, where it buried its needle-like teeth with such dexterity that Napo never awoke. When the men intervened at this point the bat leisurely flew away.

It is said that for some reason the bite of a vampire bat seldom becomes septic, healing very rapidly.

Napo had been bred in the mountains, and was young and quite inexperienced in the jungles of the Oriente. I don't think he liked them much at first.

He would bound on shore when we pulled up to a bank and disappear in the underbrush after game— promptly losing himself in the process. This disturbed him mightily, and us, too; for he would stand quite still, afraid to move, yet howling lustily until one of the Indians had cut through the underbrush and rescued him. On one occasion he went so far afield that the operation took nearly two hours.

Another morning, on embarking to set off down river, Napo was not to be found anywhere. We called and called in every direction, but no response, no answering howls in the distance to tell us his whereabouts. We were in a quandary. But abruptly a call came from an Indian who had spotted him within a few feet of us. He was lying "doggo" under a bush, motionless and soundless. My reaction was that he realized it was time to take off again, that he had become fed up with the Oriente and our whole business and wanted to go home.

However, eventually he palled up with an Indian dog which later became attached to the Expedition, and Napo soon learned all the wrinkles about jungle life from her.

At first, I thought he was a bit of a damn fool. But I was soon to change my mind. One day, while awaiting carriers on the trail, I wandered off into the bush for a look-around. Idling thoughtlessly along, I missed my direction at a river crossing. I was soon puzzling my brain to get oriented and find my way out when suddenly I turned and there was Napo.

He seemed to know my predicament at once, and with two friendly yelps to reassure me he disappeared into the jungle. Within a few minutes he had found the trail and set up an insistent barking that guided me to the others without delay.

Here he met me delightedly, quite obviously pleased with himself yet without appearing to expect thanks or to be saying, "Who's the damn fool now?"

It's a good and generous world, the dog world.

From time to time we would see tapirs, wild pigs, caymans (type of alligator), and in one case a moving head that Castillo declared was a boa. And all around us chattering parrots, toucans, and troops of monkeys.

We had already begun to hear fantastic stories about the constrictors that were said to dwell in the region of the River Curaray, the largest of which is the anaconda. The reputed size of these snakes is a gross exaggeration, for no one has ever yet secured a South American anaconda or boa constrictor much over twenty-odd feet in length. The skins exceeding this size have been greatly stretched. It is quite easy to stretch a nineteen-foot skin to twenty-three or -four feet while it is still fresh; but the deception is readily discernible. Not only are the scales on a stretched skin separated in an unnatural manner, but the markings are also distorted. Moreover, the width of the skin is another indication. A normal nineteen-foot anaconda skin will measure from thirty to thirty-six inches in width in the center; whereas a stretched skin twenty-three feet long may be less than eighteen inches in maximum width. I do not know of any authentic account of an anaconda's attacking a human being.

Snakes abound in this region, but it is astonishing how few one sees unless out especially to hunt them. Probably the most numerous of the venomous snakes in this part of the Oriente is the fer-de-lance (Equis or Pitalala). It is this snake, I believe, which was introduced to the French West Indies during slave days, the idea being that the presence of deadly snakes would prevent the slaves from running away and taking to the bush. The scheme, however, was a complete failure. Accustomed to the African jungles and their venomous snakes, the negroes had no undue dread for the fer-de-lance and were rarely bitten. Moreover, the snakes found it far easier to pick up a living about the houses, on the plantations, and in the towns than in the forests; and very soon they became a real menace to the inhabitants. Numerous persons were bitten while strolling through the gardens and parks, even in the larger cities; many deaths resulted from persons being bitten when working on the estates, and every effort was made to exterminate the deadly reptiles. But in vain. The mongoose, introduced for the purpose of killing off the fer-de-lance, preferred poultry and wild birds to snakes and soon became almost as great a nuisance as the fer-de-lance itself. The snake-eating secretary birds of Africa were next tried, but unfortunately the birds feed only during the daytime; whereas the fer-de-lance is a nocturnal reptile, and no desirable results followed this experiment. Today Martinique, St. Lucia, Grenada, and other islands are cursed by the presence of great numbers of these venomous snakes, which in some places are so abundant that whole localities have been abandoned by the people.

More deadly even than the fer-de-lance, in fact, in ways the most dangerous of all South American snakes is the "parrot snake," which is very common in certain portions of both Central and South America. It has a nasty habit of resting among thick grass and hanging vines which render it almost invisible,

and it strikes with inconceivable speed and vicious-
ness upon the least provocation. Here also dwells the
famed bushmaster.

Early one morning Vargas and several of the Indians, ahead in the canoes, fell on an unfortunate herd
of some twenty or more wild pigs which had chosen
to swim the river as we came along.

Machetes, spears, and clubs raised havoc among
them, and in the end our larder was so well replenished
that we ate wild pig until there were complaints and
protestations that unless the menu was changed there
would be wholesale desertion.

Of an evening George Brun would arouse us with
the snapping of his automatic. He would be off on the
river bank after caymans, flashing his light to attract
them to their doom, then blasting away as their but-
ton eyes broke above the surface.

It seemed difficult to realize that not so long before
we had broken in abruptly on the desultory life of
Riobamba and that only a few months previously we
had left the teeming metropolis of modern New York.

And here we were deep in the far interior of Ecuador's Oriente, with no sign of human life around us.

Over all spread an inescapable feeling of desolation
despite the riotous profusion of growing things. Our
surroundings were eerie and ominous, vast in their
silences. What a land of ghosts!

At one place a deserted house was still standing in
solitary grandeur. Quiet, forlorn, and mysterious, it
gave every evidence that it had been abandoned hur-

riedly. Within everything was in disarray. Old shoes, lamps, picture frames, chests, and broken furniture were scattered about. In a corner stood a blackboard bearing in Spanish a message written in faded chalk requesting all passers-by to respect the house and its pitiful contents "now that it is alone."

Under the high raised floor of the structure were three graves, above each a wooden cross thrust in the ground. Several withered wreaths, even an Indian headdress or two, hung on the arms of the crosses that stood above the dead. To one side was broken ground, the beginning of another tomb, and on its cross faint penciled lines still marked the space prepared for some unfilled-in name.

Even the sun's bright rays were dimmed by the gloom of the place, and I wondered what mute explanation of the hacienda's end those lonely graves could offer.

A last touch, a finis, as it were, to the sorrow of the spot, was its tragic, once ambitious name, El Porvenir—The Future!

Vicuna had been right—it was a land of "Nadie-Nadie," now given over without resistance to a world of insect and animal life.

The Curaray was proving to be a river of many twists and turns, winding its way sluggishly between the low jungle-covered banks. The river's course made such astonishing detours, or *vueltas*, that at one point it took half an hour to drift round a curve to a point only seventy yards from where we started.

Whenever possible at night we took "star sights." This is a most arduous work, and here generally can only be done between 7 P.M. and 9 P.M. at night before clouds obstruct one's vision.

First the radio must be set up to receive the *exact* time from Washington, and our chronometer checked with that. The transit in place, both the bearing and the elevation of four *different* stars in four different sectors, and four readings of *each* must be recorded.

The time of each reading must be taken by stopwatch, to the fifth of a second, and records of the temperature, humidity, and barometric pressure must be taken before and after. Add to this the adjustments that must be made for normal instrument errors, and it will be readily seen that such a performance is not carried out in a few minutes.

The days went slowly by—nothing but endless drifting down the great broad river on our two rafts, which we had long since come to look upon as home.

Now one thing you cannot do on a raft is to increase your speed, and, contrary to what some might suppose, a heavy craft will travel faster than a lighter one in the same speed of current.

George Brun knew this, I fancy, and decided to use the fact to his own advantage, for he was now very bored with our endless demands for food. Upon constructing larger rafts, which we did at one point, he purloined the heavier one, claiming that our endless piles of food supplies and cooking paraphernalia were being endangered on the smaller one. But George has a strong French accent, and I, presumably, a very English one. In the years we have known each other I don't think we have ever understood one single word the other said. We get on admirably! Consequently, whenever George asked for anything I said "yes"—I always said "yes" to George. It saved a lot of time, and George always knew what he was doing.

The next morning we were no sooner afloat, however, than I realized the bitter truth. "What the hell!" said George, and, as the stream quickly separated our two craft, the Andes-Amazon Expedition was presented with a picture of a solitary George, a delectable breakfast, and a steaming teakettle drifting far ahead round the bend.

I fancy Hector Moran must have overheard my remarks about this misunderstanding, and here was a new opportunity to shirk work which his ever fertile brain could not overlook! A French accent that even I couldn't understand—so how could he, Hector, be expected to know what George was talking about when he directed him to heavy tasks? He quite overlooked the fact that they always spoke to each other in *Spanish*.

We were now approaching the mouth of the River Cononaco, and I recalled the story of Roggierone's large expedition of a good many years before after the "Chiripuno gold."

"What is this Chiripuno gold?" John Ohman interjected. "This country seems full of stories of it."

"Yes, more full of gold legends than of the gold itself."

However, legend or not, the general belief in the existence of the gold was to cause us no little trouble later on.

The old Auca woman who had told me of the "white chief with the beard" had also remembered that the men of her tribe used to pick nuggets out of the banks of numerous creeks. Again, an Indian whom I had met had regaled me with accounts of even a greater hoard than the woman had mentioned. To his vivid imagination it was easier to find than the proverbial "gold in the streets."

It was on this quest that Roggierone had taken a large expedition up the Cononaco, into which the Chiripuno empties. The project was ill fated from the start. Resenting the intrusion upon their domain, the Aucas set upon the strangers before they could even reach their objective, split the party and inflicted terrible losses as it fled back to safety.

The expedition is still referred to as "Roggierone's Disaster," and recalling the story brought again to one's mind that grim, intangible menace of the Aucas!

The absence of the much-needed Indians, the Zaparos, decided me to leave the main party on the rafts, and to push on with a few men to Tarqui on the Peruvian frontier to arrange for the Expedition's passage to the Napo, the nearest point where we could now hope to obtain the necessary men for the completion of our program.

So I took John Ohman, Castillo, the interpreter, and Hector with me, and we quickly prepared a dug-out canoe, and mounted on it the outboard motor. Then I had an idea.

Severo Vargas' contract called for a *monthly* rate of pay. It is native custom in the interior that when one contracts for Indians for a long period of time, the period of employment is determined and paid for by the month. And so it was with Severo Vargas. He had blithely given me notice to "leave at the frontier," believing full well that before it could be reached he would be entitled under the laws of the land to more pay.

This meant for Severo, too important a man to handle a paddle himself, weeks, if not months, of pleasant, idle days on a slowly drifting raft while "good American dollars" poured into his coffers.

However, there was one thing that the old man had overlooked, or didn't know—we had an outboard motor!

Smilingly, I beckoned him toward me, ensconced him in a second canoe, and with this in tow set off downstream.

Vargas was immensely pleased at the picture of himself shooting down the Curaray in the manner of a *caballero elegante*. The fumes of the outboard were as perfume to his nostrils, and his one regret was that his friends in Puyo were not on hand to see the high station he had achieved. I held my peace.

Though it rained steadily through the day and

night, we continued our everlasting mapping and sketching as best we could. According to my diary we had covered many miles by five o'clock—a great change and a welcome one after days of slow moving by raft.

When Vargas heard what distance we had traversed, his brows knit, his smile departed, and a dawning look of comprehension spread over his face. Each mile, every twist of the river, was bringing him closer to the ruination of his well-laid schemes, to a fate of his own making.

Out of the corner of his eye he looked at me with admiration and respect. One who could outwit Severo Vargas must indeed be worthy.

But all things come to an end, and eventually we arrived at Tarqui, which consisted of only the military post on the left bank and three or four houses across from it. However, after days of utterly deserted, uninhabited jungle-covered shores, it was paradise to us.

Far more than that, we had arrived on the frontier at last, and in spite of our failure to collect ethnological specimens of the vanished Zaparos, the River Curaray, broad and deep, was all that we had hoped for. Unlike its great neighbor, the Napo, the Curaray had no rapids in its winding, tranquil course and offered everything necessary to become a great waterway of the future.

The first stage of the Expedition was now complete.

Chapter VII

THE FRONTIER OF DISPUTE AND THE CHIRIPUNO GOLD

ANTICIPATING Severo's shrewdness in the matter, I had taken him with me in the canoe, the unexpected speed of which brought us to our destination well inside the current month, for which he had already been paid. There was, therefore, nothing more due him on arrival in Tarqui; he was now in a mess of his own making because he would have to get himself and his men back up the Curaray at his own expense.

Severo Vargas was not one to take his defeat lying down. Shouting and brandishing a carbine of rusty exterior, he demanded a trial. Caramba! he would sue! Caramba! *los Americanos* were not to make a fool of him! Caramba! justice would have its day.

So we adjourned to the largest house in the settlement, a combined dwelling and military barracks. The place was thronged, but no less so than the clearing outside, where, in the manner of the Oriente, everyone, men, women and children alike, held an impromptu town meeting and discoursed long and loud, to whomever would listen, on the matter in hand. Señor Hector Moran was the only silent one. He was watchfully waiting—waiting to take sides with the winner.

Tarqui had never seen such a day, and even the monkeys for miles around seemed to be taking to the deeper bush in quaking fear.

The presiding judge was the military officer. He heard old Vargas out. He heard me out. Then he called for the contract. It took him but a moment to read the terms—and the case was thrown out of court.

Caramba! Tarqui went back to its familiar life of ease and placid conscience after a brief half hour of such pandemonium as the small village seldom knew.

Vargas hadn't a leg to stand on when that contract was shown, and the old ruffian knew it well. We shook hands outside the court without malice; and, when the great suit was finished, I know he felt no grudge at my victory. He had had a sporting chance, and it had been worth trying.

A short distance to the north, on the Napo River, lies the main frontier station of Rocafuerte. That region has been civilized and opened up for years; but so difficult is the country intervening that the only feasible way along this part of the frontier is up the Nashino and down the Yasuni Rivers. It is by this route that the headquarters at Rocafuerte supplies and administers the smaller post of Tarqui; this was the one we were to follow.

Though merely a few miles in a straight line, it is a matter of some days' journey, depending on the state of the two rivers to be traveled en route. Immediately adjacent to it was the utterly unknown territory of the truculent Aucas, running all the way along the northern bank of that river of the dead, the Curaray.

A large hacienda near the frontier on the Napo was to be my next stop; for San Miguel, the owner, was the only man on these lower rivers who was said to have enough Indians to make our entry into the Aucas' territory possible.

I was now favored by a great stroke of luck; for Major Montalvo, who was in command of all the frontier posts in the region, appeared in Tarqui; and I learned he was planning to return to Rocafuerte shortly. On hearing of my plans, he very kindly suggested that I should make the journey with him.

My departure from Tarqui impressed itself on my memory ineradicably—we actually left on schedule. This I think must be a unique event in the history of South American travel.

So, saying good-by to John Ohman, who remained temporarily with the Military Post, just before dawn, and making arrangements for the remainder of the Expedition to remain at Tarqui for further word or carriers from us, the Major and I set off.

Our route was first by trail through the jungle to the Nashino. Though muddy after the heavy rains, the trail was easy. Two hours after leaving Tarqui we arrived at our destination and found a large military canoe awaiting us.

Here at the Nashino, Aragundi, in command of the Tarqui post, left us. He had come overland to see his senior officer, Montalvo, "safely off the premises," as we would say in the British Army under similar circumstances when an inspecting officer had passed. We always politely "saw them off"—to make quite sure they had gone.

We were soon on our way, upstream, heading for a point some seven or eight days away, where a trail linking the two rivers would take us across to the Yasuni, which flows into the Napo.

The canoe was a large craft with eight or ten paddlers, and equipped with a palm leaf shelter roof as a protection against the sun and rain.

At dinner that night, Montalvo regaled me with stories of the Aucas; and, when he heard of my intention to go among them, did all he could to dissuade me. Such a venture as I proposed would take a hundred trained men, he said. Farther on, on the frontier, and on the Napo, none of the civilians wished to aid me in the scheme, and I was to learn that the feelings on the part of some *haciendieros* had become very pronounced in this respect. News had reached me that two Zaparo Indians had been located who had fought against the Ssabelas, or Aucas, and were thoroughly familiar with a river in the Auca territory where gold was to be found in great quantities. Gold! That was the cause of all the trouble. As the story developed, this river became a veritable flood of gold. The river, of course, was the famed Chiripuno, of "Roggerione's Disaster." Yet whatever I said to the contrary, however much I protested that my ambition was to meet the Aucas rather than to secure their gold, they would not change their belief. The story grew to such an extent that it was made quite clear that they believed I knew the exact location of this gold. They opposed every attempt on my part to proceed.

The Nashino proved to be an interesting river, very tropical in character. Orchids appeared to be more profuse here than on the Curaray. Game was plentiful, and an odd curassow (wild turkey) now and then helped our evening meals, which were presided over, rather, dominated by, Gringo, the Major's negro cook.

Gringo was a great character from Esmeraldas on the coast. A gigantic fellow six feet four inches in height and enormously powerful, he was totally without respect for anyone. When he had prepared a meal, you had to eat it whether you liked it or not.

We had a considerable amount of rain; and though, normally, Indians pole their canoes when going upstream, the overhanging vines of the jungle-covered banks made this difficult for our large canoe; hence we resorted to paddles.

We arrived a day late, yet with a feeling of great relief; for here a trail led overland to the Yasuni, where the military motor launch was supposed to await Montalvo.

The trail proved easy, and the next afternoon we came to the river bank, only to find that there was no sign of the launch, and when it came chugging into view that afternoon, it was too late to start for Rocafuerte.

We embarked the next morning and about noon came out into what seemed to me, after so long in restricted jungle spaces, a vast expanse of water—the Napo River. Here it is almost a mile across, and I had not focused my eyes on anything so far off as the opposite bank for several months. Turning down river towards Rocafuerte, we soon arrived at the hacienda.

The sight of a house with open pastures around it was a cheering spectacle, and I felt quite ready for our next step, up the Napo and the Aucas!

The hacienda was owned by the aforementioned San Miguel, who, with customary hospitality, insisted upon putting me up.

My anxiety was intense to know whether San Miguel would supply us with the Indians we required. Upon first meeting him I had told him of our needs. He made no answer; yet I knew he was considering my proposal. The matter could not be pressed in any way; and, in accordance with the baffling custom of the district, I had to wait and hope until he chose to bring the subject up of his own volition.

Then one afternoon he called me, and I thought that the great moment had arrived. But I was in error. He was only testing out a small consignment of curare poison, an article of commerce which varies much in quality.

Miguel was to try it out on toads, which because of their sluggish circulation can withstand it longer than most creatures. Three unfortunate toads were captured.

Jabbing each one with a blow-gun dart dipped in the curare, we awaited results. The first toad expired so quickly that I could not time it. The next escaped under the house, while the third one must have been unusually tough. After three or four minutes its sides caved in, but with a deep puffing breath it appeared to recover temporarily. This was repeated several times over a period of ten or fifteen minutes; then the toad hopped frantically across the clearing and disappeared down an abandoned well.

Most *haciendieros* keep curare in stock for their Indians, who still use the blow-gun in hunting. Their accuracy with this weapon is a source of constant wonder to newcomers.

My impatience over the delay in receiving a decision on the matter of our Indians became almost unendurable. Yet even should we have received a favorable one then, it would have required three or four weeks to bring the remainder of our baggage over to the Napo.

Throughout my stay at the hacienda stories were filtering in which disclosed strong local opposition to the Expedition's progress. At the bottom of it all was gold—the gold of the Aucas. The thing was becoming

a curse on our whole undertaking, and it availed nothing to protest that I cared nothing about it.

Then a thought occurred. If they so strongly believed that I was after their gold, I would make a
business proposition. It worked, and soon both San
Miguel and I had an important legal-looking docu-
ment in our hands, making over to him a goodly proportion of the Chiripuno hoard on the condition that
he would accompany us with his Indians.

On such an undertaking the *padron* or "owner" of
the Indians is of incalculable help. The *padron* system
is an old survival from the feudal days of the
Spaniards. The mountain Indian loves his house and
the land on which it stands. He hates to leave it; and
it has generally been granted to him in consideration
of labor by a white landowner, who therefore becomes
his *padron*.

Land has not so much of a hold on the Indians in
the Oriente. Here Indian houses are apt to be quite
temporary affairs and are constructed easily from the
timber which is ever ready at hand. Land, as such,
means nothing. You find miles of it in any direction
you go, all more or less productive if cleared and
tended. For this reason fertilizing is unnecessary.
When a patch of cultivated ground becomes sterile,
the Indian abandons it and clears a new patch in the
jungle nearby; but he is held in debt by his *padron* to
the extent of such supplies and equipment as he has
secured. Debts are paid off in work and are seldom
liquidated, even by death, unpaid debts being often

the sole inheritance. In the Oriente it is these debts rather than land that hold tremendous power over the Indians. They will do anything for their *padron,* whose good will toward an expedition, therefore, is greatly to be desired.

At the same time, the *padron's* wealth is dependent upon the number of Indians in debt to him; they are his real capital, and without them he could do nothing. This system is common to most parts of South and Central America, by no means to Ecuador alone.

Hence my relief at persuading San Miguel to accompany the Expedition in person with his Indians. Things very quickly commenced to happen. It would take some little time to assemble all the carriers necessary, but meantime Miguel dispatched a party to Tarqui to retrieve the remainder of our baggage.

I felt elated—at last everything was solved.

That evening Sonny Griswold arrived at the house from Tarqui, followed immediately by—of all people —Severo Vargas.

It appeared that Sonny had arrived in Tarqui from up the Curaray. Wanting to reach me quickly but finding no Indians at the settlement to bring him overland, and knowing nothing of my contretemps with Vargas, he had accepted the latter's graciously proffered services. This was the one chance that Vargas had needed to get himself and his Indians out of their dilemma and be paid for doing it to boot. I looked steadfastly at Severo, and our eyes met while a thousand thoughts passed between us. There was a long pause, then simultaneously we both burst out laughing. Severo Vargas had got the better of me again.

The evening grew into one of celebration in which we all took part. It was the eve of my departure, and early the next morning I was well on my way up the Napo.

Chapter VIII

FEVER

THE longer we had remained near the haciendas on the frontier, the longer the absurd chattering as to our true purposes had continued. This was not so of the more intelligent people, of course; but, when some imaginative minds set to work, the results were astounding.

So, having already arranged for the Expedition to avoid the civilized points and turn sharply westwards as soon as it arrived at the mouth of the Yasuni, I went on to await it and avoid further comment.

A few days away was a stretch of river bank once called Oasis. I had had reports of some interesting pieces of old pottery having been found there after unusually high floods. The site was not far above the Yasuni's mouth, where the Expedition would rendezvous; therefore I decided to make a camp and excavate until we should be together again.

I had engaged three Indians from San Miguel to do the digging; and these, with Hector, made up the party. Three days' travel brought us to the vicinity. Clearing a space in the jungle, we soon had our camp erected.

All went well until sundown, when, almost as if at a signal, literally clouds of mosquitoes appeared— and the bad anopheles, too. It is strange how they take to certain places and not to others, for a little farther down there had been none at all. Moreover, we were on dry, sandy soil with no sign of still water or swamps in the vicinity. These mosquitoes turned out to be the worst I had yet met with. By sundown one had to be under one's net and stay there until after dawn, but even so their never ceasing drone assailed the ears all night.

Next day we got to work on the excavating and unearthed a number of pieces of interesting design.

This work of digging up old broken pots, quite useless to cook with, was, to the Indians, the most stupid chore a white man had ever asked them to do. My pleasure was totally beyond their comprehension. They soon lost interest and, outside the lucky capture of a young deer as it was crossing the river, found life a very dull affair.

It always interests me to see the magical activity into which a group of Indians are transformed at the sight of game. So it was then. They had been digging into the bank at a pace so desultory that I imagined I was watching a scene taken by a slow-motion camera. Suddenly there was a low hiss; and one of the men indicated down stream a tiny black speck, hardly discernible to me, on the surface of the water. Instantly they dropped their shovels, took to the canoes, and went paddling furiously off at a speed that was a revelation.

Twenty minutes later they returned triumphantly, with the deer half skinned. That was the end of the day's work. Dinner became of paramount importance.

The Ssabelas had been called the "phantom Indians." Optimistically I had believed that we could study them "in our stride," as it were, by making contact with them through the Zaparos. By this time I knew to the contrary. In the course of the expedition we circumscribed their whole territory and entered its western end, but at no point do they seem to have any communication whatsoever with the outside world. Their territory is surrounded by a zone of totally un-inhabited land, and the abject terror in which they are held by such nearby semi-civilized tribes as do exist, and their own unquestionable hostility to strangers, make a friendly introduction impossible. Even the priests, who seem to go everywhere, refuse to enter their region and leave them severely alone.

Of course anyone could enter with a large armed force and drive his way in, but such a conquistador would defeat his own ends. The only feasible technique would be to camp just inside their boundaries, leave presents on their trails, and wait hopefully for their curiosity to bring them around of their own volition.

It was clear that the undertaking required a specially prepared expedition, with reliable carriers recruited from a completely different part of Ecuador, and one with that single objective alone, not with the many we were attempting.

However, I could not get the matter out of my mind. For, although we did obtain quite a few ethnological specimens now in the Museum in New York from a small remnant of three or four Zaparo families living south of the Curaray, the non-appearance of the tribe as a whole made our meager results very disappointing.

I thought again of Rayo Urcu, which I had been told many times was now the "seat of government" of the western branch of the great Ssabela tribe which was reputed to live there in "a town by a precipice beside a waterfall."

I did not believe the story, but, as all Auca attacks of recent years that I could check up on appeared to be perpetrated from the western end, I did think that some Ssabelas might be living there. It was certainly within their territory, and it was near there that Sevilla's Capricio, and other settlements had been attacked. Rayo Urcu was one of the group of hills between Napo and the headwaters of the Curaray. It was said to be a flat-topped mesa, which might afford an admirable site for an air landing field near the head of the Curaray.

It was, for those parts, reasonably easy of access and within our resources. I decided to try it.

My solitary life at Oasis was monotonous in the extreme, closely hemmed in as I was on three sides by the impenetrable jungle, with the steep river bank on the fourth. I was also on perpetual tenterhooks to know what stories were being whispered about us and the Chiripuno gold. Life was oppressive.

Sonny Griswold suddenly arrived on his way up the river. Now quite sick with fever, he was a very different Sonny from the one I had last seen. Cheerful, able to get on with anyone, he had always been a bright spark amid some very dismal moments. I was very sorry to see him go, for I felt that he would not return to the Expedition. Nor did he.

I watched Sonny disappear up the river and sat down for a smoke. When he had departed, a fearful melancholy came upon me. He had brought news that both John Ohman and George Brun had been down with the same fever that was to send him from us. I asked myself if the Expedition was beginning to crack under the pestilential climate. Was it the beginning of the end? The solitude of my jungle cubbyhole and the drone of the beastly mosquitoes seemed to say that it was.

A half hour had hardly gone by when I found myself possessed of an unreasonable lassitude. My arms were heavy; they ached to the bone. I attempted to rise. Then I knew the symptoms—fever! I had it myself.

Upon my recovery there came a break in the monotony. My nephew Alasdair appeared from out of the blue. He had left Carl and Hardwicke far back in the Llanganatis Mountains, gone out to Quito, thence by the ordinary mule trail to Napo Town on the upper river, and had come down to me in Oasis by canoe.

After a few words of greeting I soon got to the point.

"How much gold did you find?" I asked.

Alasdair shook his head. "None. And the rains are setting in up there to beat the very devil. Do you think there *is* much gold in these regions?"

"There must be some somewhere," I laughed, "if the Inca Huayna Kapac could order his goldsmiths to make a chain 700 feet long, each link as big as one's fist, to commemorate the birth of his son Huascar."

"Is that true?"

"At least it's repeated as true from many different sources. That portion of Atahualpa's ransom which was obtained by the Spaniards has been estimated by different authorities at a variable figure, according to present-day values, of from five to fifty million dollars. The King of Spain's fifth—the law of the day gave him this amount of all gold found in these newly conquered lands—of which there is definite record, included a considerable quantity of Inca articles or ornaments in their original form which leave no question of doubt as to the magnificence of their handiwork and the great quantities of gold which they must have possessed."

Several days went by and some more bad news reached me, that great pressure had been brought on Miguel's Indians by outside influences not to accompany us. This was not his fault in the least. He did not dare to fight the hostility of the river nor risk his men; so our handsome contract was not worth the paper on which it was written. This meant that the ever difficult task of getting Indians had to be done all over again. Napo Town higher up the river was my only chance, now that Miguel down below had failed.

Already two of the Indians had run away. Once this is started, a very easy thing to do, one is powerless. A few subtle lies here and there are sufficient to start a wholesale desertion—and *what* lies these were! That I would beat them, abandon them to the Aucas, steal their women; and in one instance it was actually said that I ate babies!

The imaginative Indian mind will accept such nonsense with the straightest of faces, and it soon spreads in all directions. I was now fearful that I might not even get the Expedition up the river at all, much less obtain men for Rayo Urcu. But Miguel did agree to do that, and I was much relieved when it finally started up the Napo, leaving me free to hasten on to Napo Town.

I had feared an attempt at "marooning" the Expedition's equipment. This is an old game in certain interiors. You ask for natives to take your baggage up river. There are some but not quite enough. How-

ever, they will take you up to X—— where there are
"plenty of Indians," your remaining equipment to
be sent on after you.

But upon arriving at X—— you find, if anyone at
all, a feeble old man, a sick woman, and a baby in
arms. Meanwhile even those Indians you have slip
quietly off down river, having completed their contract. This continues all the way, your baggage getting less and less until it finally disappears altogether
—strung out over miles of the country. Of course
most of your possessions left behind never arrive. They
have been "regrettably lost." Unable to obtain new
equipment in such places, the expedition precipitately
comes to an end.

When I reflect upon the quantity of baggage and
supplies we had and the great distances we covered, it
astonishes me to recall that outside of a little pilfering
we lost practically nothing of value.

Now that the Expedition was safely on the move
up river from the frontier, we took immediate steps
to leave Oasis. Securing a canoe and three Indians with
great difficulty, Alasdair, Hector, and I went on ahead,
up the Napo River, to make another attempt to obtain Indians to accompany the Expedition into Rayo
Urcu.

We had not gone far, however, before our canoe-
men vanished, leaving us stranded. This meant another
day lost, then another and another, in the usual way.
Obtaining a fresh canoe from a settler, we continued,
but the same thing happened again.

Two more days were lost, but we eventually got away again with all possible speed. It was now all-important to reach Napo Town as soon as possible, for the "influence" was evidently creeping up and eventually would reach that place. I had to get there first, and I forced the Indians ahead.

I say "forced," but this is not the correct term, for it is beyond the bounds of human possibility to "force" an Indian to do or not to do anything. No race on earth has so completely mastered the art of passive resistance as the South American Indian.

Nothing can hurry them when they do not want to be hurried; nothing can match them in nervous energy once they make up their minds to proceed elsewhere. This gives one a feeling of great helplessness when undertaking something in the jungle with which they are not in accord.

"Can he handle Indians?" is one of the first questions asked of a white man applying for a job, and is a very important one.

To those unacquainted with the subject, the approved method of handling Indians may seem harsh. But it must be remembered that as a rule the Indian is totally lacking in what we ourselves call ambition. Materials for his house and sufficient food to support him and his family can be produced within ten yards of where he is sitting. If not he sits in another place. Besides this, he appreciates a knife and machete, and once in a while a little pot of curare or other gadget to help him in his hunting. And that's about all. Consequently he doesn't want money; therefore he doesn't want to work.

No doubt there is quite a lot to be said for his point of view. But in spite of this type of labor the South American *haciendiero* is roundly criticized by us northerners for laziness if he doesn't build empires overnight.

As a matter of fact it is astonishing how much a *haciendiero* can get out of his Indians. It is rare to find any gringo who can do as well.

There's a great knack to handling Indians and one that comes far easier to some than to others, depending on their natures. It is easy, and quite a relief, to stand up to one's full height, trust in the British Army, and explode with a paroxysm of wrath. But of course that doesn't work at all. True, an Indian might aggravate you intentionally once in a while just to brighten up an otherwise dull afternoon; but that is rare. The odds are he won't connect your, to him, astonishing demonstration of fury with any act of his own at all, and will possibly commiserate with you in your anguish. Nevertheless, taken all in all he's a darned good fellow, the Indian. I like him.

To my surprise, even here on this civilized river the fear of the Aucas was not inconsiderable. I found that passing canoes, even large ones carrying six to eight paddlers, camped at night only on the northern bank to be away from the Aucas' side. This seemed ridiculous to me, for I was convinced that the center of the Auca territory must be quite a distance away.

One night in camp on a sandbank beside the river I was awakened by a strange, slithering sound. As a variation from the Aucas, the Indians had been telling hair-raising stories of the enormous boa constrictors which were reputed to seize unwary travelers sleeping on sandbanks too close to the water.

Good Lord!—we were on a sandbank. I sat up with a start. A boa? It was getting closer and closer.

Should I awaken Alasdair? He was sleeping perilously near the sound.

I reached for my flashlight, and its long beam of light shot out across the sand to disclose a dim shapeless mass. It was one of our Indians, quite unmoved. He was calmly shoving our canoe from the shore where it had grounded during the night with the receding river.

Each time it moved it gave out that alarming, slithering sound.

The incident left me wide awake, and I recalled various occasions when I had witnessed a real panic for no greater reason than a simple occurrence such as this. In India once, marching amid clouds of dust in the dim light before dawn, a whole regiment, suddenly aroused out of its drowsiness, skipped clear off the road. One officer drew his sword.

For some moments dead silence reigned. What dread thing was about to occur? What frightful monster was coming? Nothing but a cow sleeping quietly in the middle of the road!

The first two sections of fours had come upon this

apparition, but, seeing what it really was, merely stepped to one side to avoid it. The next few ranks were unable to see what it was, yet automatically stepped aside to conform with the movement of the men ahead. In the darkness this action became quicker and quicker as it went down the ranks until, in a flash, the whole regiment was flying helter-skelter off the road. It was some moments before even the Colonel could recover from his astonishment sufficiently to blaspheme adequately.

We continued wearily up the Napo River in our canoe, which was too small to carry the overhead grass shelter so often used as a protection against the sun.

To be frank, this absence of a grass roof didn't bother me, however; they are my pet abomination. A dugout canoe is in no case a Simmons mattress to lie on, but this fact of itself is not sufficient for the South American Indian, who, I am convinced, must sit up nights thinking out new ways and means of making already uncomfortable travel more uncomfortable.

Left to himself he will carefully erect the overhead shelter at a height above the canoe floor that scarcely permits the entry of a self-respecting weasel. Under this one is expected to travel for days and days. I recall one such journey which I was compelled to take in company with my host's wives, friends, a small party of miscellaneous women and children, and a handful of dogs.

To my companions, the restricted space was no

hardship; and the grass roof was a real luxury. But I am a tall man. When I attempted to place myself in the seat provided, hemmed in by that conglomeration of humanity, I found it impossible either to sit upright or to lie down. At the end of the first day I found myself giving the whole problem considerable thought, but I never did quite succeed in solving it.

The best I could do was to balance myself precariously on the small of my back, my left arm and nether end flapping in mid-air, and my head forced back at an angle of 30° above the horizontal which, I must concede, did have some support—on the point of a stick.

My Indian friends thoroughly enjoyed the whole excursion, but as for me, every bone in my body ached, a torment set in that seemed to continue for an eternity. It was so dark inside that I could neither read nor write, but only reflect bitterly on what the explorer, G. M. Dyott, once said to me during one of his expeditions as he eyed my six feet two acidly: "Tall men are a great nuisance. They don't fit normal store equipment; their beds have to be longer, therefore heavier; they perpetually knock things down from the tent roof with their heads, and besides"— with a stony glare at me—"they are apt to eat more!"

Commander Dyott is a very short man.

Chapter IX
INDIAN TROUBLE

OF recent years there have been many outbreaks of fever in the region of the Upper Napo and its tributaries. Many hundreds of Indians have died in the course of these scourges, which, in some cases, have caused the ruin and end of some of the large haciendas. Although at times rumors reached us of yellow fever, Dr. Wolcott, of the Rockefeller Foundation, who made a tour of inspection of the district, assured me that he had found no such cases. Rather had he found pernicious malaria.

The semi-civilized Indians are in dread of pernicious malaria; for they have, to a certain degree, lost the medicinal knowledge of the old tribes and are glad to put themselves in the hands of their *padrones* for treatment. It is the custom that such treatment and medicines are free.

Passing the estate Vargas Torres, now abandoned to the jungle, we reached Venezia, a once splendid hacienda with one of the finest houses on the river, now also abandoned. We arrived at sunset and found a scene of past grandeur. The large house with its avenue was surrounded by sheds and out-buildings, decrepit and forlorn. The nearby orange groves and gardens were now overrun by weeds and brush and were rapidly becoming lost forever. The only signs of human life were a few miserable Indians, one of whom was dying of fever.

Our men refused to spend the night in the place, preferring the questionable pleasure of hard beds on the rocky beach. It was a dismal scene; and the forsaken house, given over now to sickness, bats, and ghosts of the past, seemed supinely to accept its fate.

I reflected upon the havoc that the present high price of gold has wrought on the Napo. Depending largely in previous years on its agricultural products, it had been a busy river with many Indians working along its banks. But now the premium on gold offers an easy way to earn a living. Many of the creeks and bends in the river carry fine gold in minute quantities. Yet a few hours' panning a day will produce enough for the Indian to live on. He sells it to the *padron* for a little money or exchanges it for trade goods.

The next day we passed a party washing gold, and Señor Hector became tremendously excited. Eventually he talked them into giving him a real miner's pan in place of the Expedition's frying pan, which he had been surreptitiously using in an effort to get rich quick. He obtained a small speck of the precious stuff;

but, while looking at it, I let it drop, and it was gone forever.

Hector burst into tears. I had robbed him of a fortune, and immediately he gave notice of leaving.

Giving notice was one of Hector's strongest traits. He would wake me up at night on a solitary sandbank, miles from anywhere, without a canoe or other means of transportation in sight for days, and give notice of leaving at once. Going down a rapids with everyone desperately straining to protect the canoe and its all-important baggage, he would stop proceedings and give notice. It was only when I swore at him once and told him if he ever gave notice again I would fire him that he desisted.

But Hector had a touch of genius in achieving his own ends with the Indians. I don't know what lies he told them, but I am sure he used his status on the Expedition as a powerful lever. Furthermore, he was apt to speak to them in the majestic "we."

Offered a piece of monkey meat to eat one night when there was also a bit of turkey lying alongside it, Hector said loftily, "We white men don't eat monkey" and promptly grabbed the turkey. And at that very moment I myself was eating monkey!

A few miles above Venezia we passed the whirlpool of Latas where, we were told, a German on his way down river with a quantity of gold had capsized. The men of the area still talk of the "vast fortune" lying on the bottom of the whirlpool.

On January 8, 1936, twelve days after leaving Oasis, we arrived at Napo Town, a cleared square with about ten houses around it, where food supplies were scarce and prices very high.

Eagerly setting to work to get Indians to enter the Auca country, I headed for the house of Samuel Souder, an old North American who lived fifteen minutes' walk outside the settlement.

Souder was a Spanish-American War veteran, and in the course of his life had drifted about to many different parts of South America, finally settling down in the Oriente of Ecuador. Long, lean, a typical Yankee in appearance, he needed only a goatee, a tail coat, and a top hat to be the counterpart of Uncle Sam.

Truculent as a fighting cock, continually blaspheming other people or things that "molested" him, he could, however, be most agreeable to anyone he liked. His cussing was largely a manner of speech, for underneath he was a very kind old man. This was especially evident in his dealings with his Indians, who adored him, and he was just as fond of them.

When I arrived, an Indian was dying of dysentery on the verandah. Souder was both berating him and giving him medical treatment at the same time, and the Indian appreciated both acts equally.

Souder was interested in our project to go to Rayo Urcu; and, although he did not commit himself at once, he began to think it over.

After several tantalizing changes of mind he gave

way, and agreed to lend me his Indians, who were "on a holiday" at their *chakras* (plantations) near the mouth of the Arajuno, a tributary of the Napo. Sending word down river for the oncoming Expedition to join me there, I proceeded to the Arajuno camp to await it and Souder's Indians. At the last moment only one canoe could be obtained; so I was compelled to take the same one that was going farther down river with the message for the Expedition.

Consequently we were dumped out on a sandbank, the only available camping ground, near the Arajuno's mouth. This was cut off from shore by a narrow arm of the river quite safe at low water, but on these treacherous rivers it is a basic rule of safety not to stay in such a spot without a canoe for a quick get-away if necessary. But we had no alternative, and so, accompanied by Hector and Garces, an employee of Souder's, I landed.

The next day, however, the Indians did not appear; nor the next day, nor the day after that. The heat and flies on that bare parched sandbank became unbearable. Moreover it was now so long since I had left the Expedition that my thin supply of food, traveling light as I was, had dwindled to almost nothing. Soon we were down to a few dried plantains a day each. Worse than this, the stock of quinine had now about given out. When days passed and the Indians failed to appear, I began to believe the "Influence" had reached Souder's men also. And so it turned out, for I later discovered they had been sent a message to have no truck with me. One straightforward word from them that they would not go would have saved all that long wait on the sandbank.

Then suddenly I was heartened, for George Brun came up the river, having made good time ahead of the slower moving group because he had the outboard motor. He brought a few supplies and some quinine. George also brought news of the Expedition, which was now well on its way. They had had many delays and troubles; and both John and George had been sick, but now had quite recovered.

Previous to this, Alasdair had come down with an obstinate attack of fever. No treatment we could give would stay it, and he was compelled to leave for the higher altitudes and thence home.

That night Garces came down with fever, which, in spite of our new supply of quinine, grew rapidly worse and, to add to our troubles, after darkness set in the river suddenly began to rise. Although it was not yet raining where we were, there must have been a downpour higher up in the mountains.

The speed with which these rivers rise is astonishing. In talking over the dangers of this, Garces, who knew the river well, dismissed any chance of the sandbank's being submerged.

However, the river crept up foot by foot. Why these things so often have to happen at night, when darkness adds to one's difficulties, is one of Nature's mysteries.

Soon the arm which cut us off from the shore was

swollen to a torrent. Crossing it by the thin beam of a flashlight, with a sick man, was a great risk; yet one we might be compelled to take.

Then the rain broke, chilling George and me to the bone as we took up posts on opposite sides of Garces' bed, periodically flicking our flashlights anxiously to watch the ever rising flood. On and on it came, and the moment was at hand when we would have to risk his life to save him from certain death in the now torrential stream. Wrapping him up in what water-proofs we had, we sat waiting till the last possible moment. But the water remained level for a half hour of dire anxiety—then, to our relief, began to recede.

When dawn broke, the river was rapidly falling, and we could see the crest had reached a level only four inches below where Garces' bed had been.

A few days later Souder wrote that he could do nothing further about his Indians; so we returned to Napo.

I tried again with another *haciendiero*. Picking twenty-one willing Indians, we prepared to get under way. But before they could leave they underwent a change of heart. All the wives got sick the same day, and what was a man to do!

I began to lose hope, when a *Commandante* and his soldiers arrived to commandeer Indians for the trans-portation of a military relief to the frontier post at Rocafuerte.

To the Indians anything, even Aucas, was better than being commandeered, and they appeared with miraculous speed and a great anxiety to join our party —on the same day if possible. So Souder closed up his house and with his Indians came down river with us to the old camp. Hardly had we arrived when the remainder of the Expedition appeared from down river and the skies at once brightened.

Then suddenly Peter Prime came down with fever; and after a few days of sickness he left, going up river by canoe, on his way to the outside and New York.

There was another member of the Expedition whom I was now forced to count out of the picture for what one might call "general inadequacy." This was Señor Hector Moran. If only I could have him for the sake of George Brun! But I knew it was now impossible to keep him longer. We were shortly to enter the Auca country and later face the rigorous climate of the Llanganatis, which he would be unable to stand. His time had come.

The thought of losing the most colorful member of the group was truly distressing, and I was looking forward to our parting of the ways with a lump in my throat, my heart full of lead. However, the final interview, which I approached with great reluctance, took a sudden unexpected turn that absolved me from responsibility.

It was all over a rooster!

For some time past, I had been carefully saving an age-old rooster for a grand feast when we should at last be setting out for Rayo Urcu. The moment had now arrived, and I told Hector to kill the bird and broil it. Hector proceeded to do this in the manner with which I was long familiar. He promptly let the bird escape and sat down philosophically as it scuttled into the jungle, with the full intention of staying there for life. Hector turned to send a party of Indians, otherwise occupied upon important Expedition work, after the wretched cock.

"Get that rooster!" I roared with wrath.

An hour passed. The bird was still at large and Hector sulking.

"Get that— Not another meal do you get till you catch that bird." And I strode away.

This was a quandary from which Hector had but one avenue of escape. Ignoring my past warning, he took the whole matter into his own hands in three words: "I give notice!"

I answered in two. "I accept!"

It was all very tragic.

But Hector forgot and forgave for, months after the close of the Expedition, he wrote me a long, well-phrased letter expressing his extreme thankfulness for my safe return, his earnest hopes for my good health, a long and a happy future. He then came to the point: "Please send those many photographs you must have taken of me on the trip."

He wanted enlargements—with a sepia finish!

Chapter X
TRAILING THE PHANTOM SSABELAS

OUR eagerness to find the Aucas was whetted continually by the tales our Indian helpers kept elaborating for our benefit. The town of Rayo Urcu was really a fortress, they said, with heavy tree trunks placed ready to roll down on anyone who approached. The chief was a huge man, larger than myself, exceedingly muscular, and so agile that by leaping about he could evade a rifle bullet. He also had a beard, light skin, and a face bedecked with feathers stuck through his nose and cheeks. But these descriptions are models of plausibility compared to most we were favored with.

As luck would have it, Souder fell and sprained his wrist and could not accompany us farther. This left only John Ohman, George Brun, myself, and Castillo, the interpreter, the latter well accustomed to the bush and a man of courage and great energy.

After leaving Souder in January, we proceeded up the River Arajuno accompanied by thirty of his Indians. For a time we were followed by their women, who howled and wailed miserably that they would never see their men again. It was quite depressing. However, I don't think the men take this sort of demonstration seriously, nor even the women, for that matter. Be that as it may, the general effect, on a rainy morning, was none too cheerful.

As the day wore on the weather cleared; and after a few hours we went ashore, scaled a steep hill, and were able to get a clear view of the surrounding country. Late in the afternoon we reached a small creek and enjoyed a bath, after which we all felt in the best of spirits.

The next day we came to the junction of the Nushino and Sotano Rivers. (The Nushino is not to be confused with the Nashino far away on the frontier.) It was near here that Sevilla had been surprised and attacked by the Aucas.

The Sotano was a pleasant stream, and after looking carefully for any strange footprints, our men had a grand time spearing fish. In the midst of this one of the men called me and pointed out a matamata turtle almost submerged in a pool of mud. It snapped at us upon approach, and every time it did so we heard a low gurgling sound and smelled a foul stench. This creature has a villainous-looking diamond-shaped head with a ferocious expression, and a neck almost as long as the body. The Indians hate these turtles and think that they are devils; but I was delighted to find this one to add to our collection of zoological specimens. With some difficulty we managed to capture it alive.

After fording the Nushino we camped on the far shore. As we were now inside the Aucas' territory, guards were necessary at night. In fact the whole camp was formed into a quadrangle with a sentry on each face. We ourselves divided up the night watches from 7 P.M. to 6 A.M. equally, so that one white man was on the alert all the time. There was no trouble keeping the sentries awake.

The next day upon breaking camp I found that the precious matamata turtle had been deliberately allowed to escape, the Indians believing him an unlucky companion for an enterprise such as the one we were on. After I finished telling them what I thought of them, I think they would gladly have exchanged me for the turtle.

We pushed up a shallow creek flowing from the direction of a very large hill which we had seen in the distance and which could only be Rayo Urcu. It was easier to splash up the middle of the creek than to cut our way through the bush, although a surprise would have been harder to guard against. Fortunately the bush here was not thick, and it became thinner as we progressed. Nothing happened during the day, save an encounter with a ferocious-looking snake which the Indians asserted stings with its tail. This erroneous but quite common belief probably comes from the snake's habit of swinging its body and tail forward as it bites, rather than strikes, its victim, the habit being due to the deeply receded position of its fangs.

As the day went on we left the creek, and branched off up a low spur which we hoped would lead to the top of Rayo Urcu. The bush was now extremely sparse, and we made a comfortable camp until midnight. During my watch, a torrential downpour came on which continued until dawn. It was now February and the rainy season could be expected.

Nothing had disturbed us as yet, but we did not relax our vigilance. Rather, we became more watchful; for the next morning we came upon the first sign of the Aucas—a twig twisted over and under, instead of straight over as is the custom of the semicivilized Indians.

It was old, however, as were other similar ones we found later that day. The scarcity of these and the absence of any signs of habitation put strong doubts in my mind as to their denoting anything more than the passage of a few hunting parties through this area. That belief was strengthened when later on we came upon signs of a hunting shelter and a vine bitten through, apparently by some hunter whose hands were probably fully occupied with his loads.

Finally, on February 18th, we reached the top of the hill, and the next day set out to explore it. It was a large expanse, flat as a lawn, scantily covered with shrubs, and well drained. As it extended for a considerable distance to the east and west, it made an excellent site for the landing field which had been one of our original quests. Thus another of our aims was accomplished.

During the afternoon we came upon a tapir trail and not far from it human tracks, both far fresher than the previous signs we had seen. But these led to nothing, as the trail went over the rim of the hill and disappeared.

Here we made camp and sent out scouting parties, which returned empty-handed, however. By striking across to the south side, we found the source of the Zapino River. I recalled the old Zaparo of the three at Puerto Tunghurahua who had been driven out of this, the place of his birth, by the Aucas years ago. But still there were no signs of them, despite a dozen side trips we made into the immediate vicinity.

The next day was to be our last, for it was useless to wait longer. As there was only one end of the hill we had not yet covered, we headed in that direction and there found a precipice. Here the face of Rayo Urcu was almost perpendicular, and I recalled that the town of the legend was said to be at the top of a precipice.

Almost immediately a few hundred feet farther on towards the south we found a creek, the only water we had yet seen on top of the flat hill. Following the creek along to the edge of the precipice, we peered carefully over the brink; and there it fell fully one hundred and fifty feet, forming, presumably, the cataract of the story.

For the moment my hopes soared, but a thorough

search revealed nothing unusual on top of the hill. A careful inspection through my glasses of the floor of the plain below revealed nothing significant. I saw no signs of *chakras*, smoke, roofs of huts, or of any other signs of habitation. Yet, leaving nothing to chance, we clambered down. Our reward was only virgin jungle. There were no signs of any houses whatever, nor any suggestion that houses had ever been there. So far as any visible indications were concerned, we were the first human beings who had ever visited the spot.

The "town" of the Auca legend was a myth.

There was nothing to be done now but to bow to the inevitable. Time was getting on, and the rains were due to break. Now that we had laboriously clambered down to the base of the cliff, it was easy to utilize the Nushino, which flowed not far away, for transportation. Just before sundown we reached its banks and went into camp.

By 9 A.M. the next morning we had constructed sufficient balsa rafts from trees found near at hand to serve for our short trip down the river. The rain of the previous night and early morning helped us on our journey, for the current had risen just enough to speed our passage.

One by one the clumsy craft shoved off. Turning a bend, I came upon John Ohman doing an adroit trapeze act on an overhanging branch of a tree under which his raft had run, leaving him suspended in mid-air. At such moments John was apt to revert to his mother language—Swedish—as his most fluent medium of expression.

The rains had now set in in earnest, but soon afterwards we reached the point where I planned to leave the Nushino and take to the bush, as I wished to explore more of the country to the east, where, I now felt, the Ssabelas' true center lay.

When I explained this to the Indians, they refused on the spot. A considerable amount of their original willingness to accompany me had come from the desire to avoid being commandeered for service at Napo. The danger had now passed, and they wanted no more of *los gringos,* in spite of the fact that we had seen nothing of the dreaded Aucas.

Moreover, the precious chicha, on which they depended so much during treks like this, was beginning to give out. Yet after considerable argument the older men agreed to come along after they had replenished their supply in Napo. Since this was a familiar trick to get away, I called for volunteers with promises of extra presents and obtained eight young fellows scarcely more than boys. However, within an hour one of these deserted; and another, while chasing monkeys, fell and hurt his hand so severely that he had to go back with the main body of the Indians.

Thus short-handed again—and what a familiar experience this was becoming—I was forced to leave most of our equipment behind in a reserve camp.

We headed east, and soon reached a hill which overlooked the Ssabela country. Felling some trees and clearing away brush, we made a fine observation post from which, with the aid of glasses, we studied the geography of the area.

Far ahead rose a mass of hills stretching from the valley of the Curaray right across to the Napo River. Here, without doubt, was the Ssabela center, for their river, the Chiripuno, flows eastward into either the Cononaco or the Tiputini (there is a controversy on this point locally) and must consequently rise on the eastern slopes of the hills we saw before us.

We had now learned a lot about the Aucas' territory. The country ahead of us was dense jungle which would require days to get through, the project requiring, moreover, a completely reorganized and re-equipped party. The whole undertaking, because of the lack of available semi-civilized Indians, would be by no means an easy nut to crack.

Chapter XI
"THE WORST PEOPLE ON EARTH"

BEFORE leaving New York I had endeavored to obtain all the facts available regarding the tribes in this region. It was easy enough in the case of the Quechua races or the head-shrinking Jivaros. But when it came to the Ssabelas it was a different matter. The only book I could find that even mentioned them was that of Gunther Tessman, who had not been in the territory. The origin of their name, Ssabela, was a puzzle which even he could not solve.

As a matter of fact, locally I seldom heard the word "Ssabela" applied to them; in fact, no true name at all, only appellations of obvious meaning, such as "Aucas" (meaning wild people), "Salvaches" (corruption of "savage"), "Aushiris" (incorrect, for the true Aushiris live further down the Curaray River in Peru), "Chiripunos" (from the name of the river they are said to dwell upon), and "Puca-Aucas" (red-footed Aucas) from their supposed custom of staining their feet as well as their bodies with red pigment.

Eventually I was fortunate enough to gather considerable information about Ssabelas. The best explanation of the name "Ssabela" that I heard was given by one Javier Davalos, an old Indian who at one time had lived on the outskirts of their country.

About 1910, he said, he was on the borders of the Ssabela district near Tibacuno, accompanied by some Quechua-speaking Indians. These managed to make friends with members of a small sub-tribe of "Aucas" known as the Wabos. Unlike their savage kinsmen, the Wabos were not very hostile; and Davalos induced a Wabo woman to work for him.

After a couple of months, however, she decamped and rejoined her tribe, later to return to Davalos, in whose employ she remained for several weeks. Then she again vanished. As was customary among the *padrones* of the Oriente, Davalos gave her a Spanish name, in this case, Isabella. This was transformed to "Ssabela" by the Quechua-speaking Indians in his employ. The result was that she became known by that name throughout the area.

Although she never again returned to work for the old Indian, she remained on friendly terms, and together with a few men of her tribe, frequently met the Quechua Indians, who always referred to this particular band of "Aucas" as "the men of Ssabela," and finally as "Ssabelas." As I could find no one who recalled the name "Ssabela" as being applied to the tribe until twenty or twenty-five years ago, and as they are still called "Aucas" by the majority of the people of Ecuador, it may be quite possible that Davalos' explanation of its origin is the right one.

Davalos could give no estimate of the numbers of the tribe. Like others with whom I talked, he could only say they were "very strong in numbers"; and I have heard estimates of anything from one to ten thousand. However, all persons who seemed to have any knowledge of them agreed that they dwell in large community houses accommodating fully fifty persons, with thatched roofs extending to the ground and a door at each end. It was also agreed that the houses are rectangular and not elliptical, as are those of the Jivaros, and the general belief was that they live in "towns," which if true is exceptional for these parts.

All reports also agreed that the Aucas go nude, not even wearing G-strings or breech cloths, although during dances, ceremonials, and on other occasions they adorn themselves with feather headdresses, feather and thread amulets, and decorate their bodies with variously colored clays. They also use ear plugs of hard baked clay, which are so heavy that they frequently stretch the ear lobes to the shoulders. In the case of women the ear plugs are used only after marriage. Both sexes also insert two long feathers through perforations in the sides of their noses, tying the quills together beneath the nostrils so that the plumes project beyond the cheeks at an angle of about forty-five degrees. Both sexes also perforate the lower lip and wear pendants or ornaments of monkey teeth in the incision.

It was also said that at ordinary times a plain wooden pin is worn in the hole in the lower lip and that while talking they move this about with their tongues, a habit which is also common to the Jivaros.*

One report which greatly astonished me was that all who had actually seen the Aucas declared them to be very light-colored—"as light as you are." The women, I was informed, are even lighter (I was deeply tanned at the time); the men usually large and stout, with long hairs staggered at the temples. Although addicted, according to reports, to the use of chicha, the Aucas never become intoxicated.

One of my informants declared that the men are monogamous but that the chiefs have two wives, that there are no concubines, and that marriage between near relations is considered a grave sin.

Davalos described their marriage customs, stating that the prospective groom must show his skill by stabbing his spear through a slender stick, and if he fails to hit the mark, he is not deemed worthy of marriage. During the ceremony, which is often held for

---

* According to some authorities these customs indicate decidedly Carib tendencies. The low-roofed rectangular community houses, the ear plugs and the feathers in the nose as well as the perforated lower lip are all in vogue among the various tribes of Carib stock throughout the Guianas, Venezuela, Brazil, Peru, Bolivia, Colombia, and elsewhere.

It would be interesting to learn if the Aucas decorate their foreheads or heads with tufts of white down attached to the hair. This is the tribal mark of the Caribs and might be conclusive evidence that the Ssabelas are of Carib stock.

a number of weddings at once, the men dance in one group and the women in another. As the dance proceeds, both groups push together until the men finally force the women into their hammocks. The elders or medicine men then stand over the couples and instruct them as to married life and duties.

The Ssabelas do not use bows and arrows but depend entirely upon their long, heavy, hardwood spears for warfare. The blades, which are almost as hard as iron, have numerous barbs cut along the edges so that they are usually left behind in the wound, the Ssabelas taking pride in thus demonstrating their disregard for their weapons. If withdrawn from the wound the barbs lacerate the flesh fearfully; but I do not think the spears are poisoned.

In reality these spears are more properly javelins and are thrown with great accuracy up to a distance of a dozen yards or so, which is ample in the jungle. As a rule, the first spear is aimed at the victim's abdomen, thus disabling him, the subsequent spears being hurled at the mouth, throat, and chest. Even after the man is dead, they drive numerous spears into his body, leaving them as proof of their numbers and strength.

For hunting, and hunting only, these Indians employ the blow-gun and darts treated with a deadly poison said to be even more terrible than the famous curare, although it does not retain its potency for so great a length of time.

If, as several persons assured me, the Ssabelas' blowguns are rectangular instead of round in section, they differ materially from those of any other Indians of South America that I have met.

I was also told by Carlos Sevilla and others that the Ssabelas possess "watching birds." According to him the Quechua name of these birds is *Acangao*. They are black with white breast and red quills. I have seen numbers of these birds on the Arajuno River. In captivity they are said to utter loud cries of warning when any stranger approaches.

One unusual fact which came to me from many sources was the Ssabelas' abhorrence of eating salt. They believe that the reason other people are bad is because of the salt they eat. I have heard it said that their custom is to bleed a newly captured child of another tribe many times, to remove all traces of the obnoxious stuff from the child's system. This dislike appears most exceptional, for Indians and animals alike will go to the most extreme trouble to obtain salt if deprived of it. It is possible that the vegetables of the Ssabelas contain a natural sufficiency of this to supply their bodily needs without their being aware of it.

Another interesting custom, which on Rayo Urcu I had found to be true, was that, whereas the other Indians when traversing the jungle break obstructing twigs and branches straight over and away from themselves, the Ssabelas twist the twigs backwards and then underneath in the direction in which they are going.

As I have said, Davalos knew more about these "Phantom Indians" than any man I met, but I also secured some very interesting information from an Auca woman named Juana, whom I found at Napo.

When about fourteen years of age she had been captured by a rubber gatherer who brought her to his camp, on the Napo River. She was a pronounced type with a strong facial resemblance to certain North American Indians. She had a narrow head with a rather broad face and very high cheekbones, small narrow eyes placed far apart, a long straight nose, straight rather full lips, strong jaws and fine teeth.

She could give little information regarding the rivers of her tribe's district but told me that she had lived somewhere near a large Auca "town" with many houses larger than that in which we were seated.

As this was the priest's house, thirty or forty feet in length and fully twenty-five feet in height, the Aucas' houses are truly very large if Juana's memory can be relied upon.

Moreover, she declared that the "town" contained so many houses that it extended as far as from the River Napo to Souder's house, a distance of nearly a mile! This I certainly don't believe.

Very often, she told me, she had been taken quite a distance from her home, accompanied by men or women of her tribe, on visits to other Indians. Sometimes, also, they went to a creek beyond a marsh, where they picked up lumps of gold which they sometimes used as ornaments or "to play with."

Fire, she said, was kindled by twirling a stick between the hands, the pointed end resting upon a piece of wood upon which had been placed tinder made of pulverized dried leaves.

Pointing to my beard, I asked if she had ever seen such a thing among the Auca men. She assured me she had and added that all three of the headmen she had known wore beards like mine, but that none of the ordinary men had them.

Her parents had told her that her tribe had come originally from farther down the Amazon Valley to the east and that an elderly curaca had stated that once the members of the tribe had worn some sort of garments which for some unexplained reason had been wholly discarded.

Owing to the fact that Juana spoke very poor Spanish and that even Castillo had difficulty in understanding her, it was not easy to obtain very detailed accounts of her people and her girlhood.

She was very childish and light-hearted, although nearly forty years of age when I talked with her. She giggled most of the time, and at first appeared greatly ashamed of the fact that she was an Auca. In fact, she had almost completely forgotten her own language and could only give me a few words, among which were: Inkimo (egg), Nainke (sun), Ukabo (head), and Hopa (water).

Chapter XII
THE LOST MINES OF THE INCAS

IT WAS now seven months since we had left New York, and the time had come to leave the Oriente.

Now remained the last and major stage—the exploration of the Llanganatis Mountains. The fact that the rainy season had just commenced was a bad feature, but it was impossible to keep a large expedition waiting idly in the field for many months. My original plan had been to undertake this by December, but through the unavoidable delays and constant inability to obtain Indians in the Oriente, etc., it was now either to go into the mountains despite the rain or abandon the project until another year.

We closed our affairs at Napo Town and cleared up the various financial details that a large expedition like ours always gets involved in.

The next step was to proceed by canoe, then overland on foot in order to strike the mule trail at Mera. Here we were in familiar territory, and with each step ahead we began to forget the heat and flies we had

John Ohman, Captain E. Erskine Loch, and George Brun Among
the Hostile Ssabela Indians, after Six Months in the Field

Above: A Condor, the Glory of the Andes, with George Brun
Below: The Rare Hairy Tapir
Note the White Tips on Ears and Lips

known farther east on the Curaray. From Mera we proceeded on muleback, and what a relief it was after the cramped quarters of the previous months in canoes and on rafts.

Who should appear en route but Bill Klamroth, fresh from gold mining in Puerto Rico.

"I just dropped in to see what was going on," was his explanation.

His arrival brought our party up to four in all. Castillo, the interpreter, had already left. His services in the Oriente had been an invaluable help to the Expedition; but in the mountains they were no longer required.

In New York, during the organization, I had watched Bill Klamroth embark for Puerto Rico and had not imagined that I would see him again—or at least not until my return to New York. But, as it turned out, Bill was to be in constant association with me and remained with the Expedition from this time on until its close. Six feet four, of immense nervous energy and physical endurance, he had an unusually good memory for country. He could find his way anywhere—and back again, which is not always the same thing. He was a most valuable addition to the Expedition.

At this time I received a letter from Carl de Muralt, who had left us months before to follow the gold trail of the "Derrotero" with Montford Hardwicke. The sum and substance of the letter was that they had found no gold, and Hardwicke had already returned to the States. Carl was planning to follow him almost immediately.

We soon reached Pillaro, where we arranged a base from which to launch our attack on the Llanganatis.

Once we were established, the others joined me with that part of our heavy equipment we had left in Ambato months before; and we set about the task of renewing clothing and food supplies, and generally re-equipping for the mountains.

This meant a complete change in attire, camp paraphernalia, etc., from what we had carried into the hot Oriente. Now we should need heavy sheepskins for the high altitudes, different types of condensed foods, waterproofs in abundance, and heavy sleeping bags, to name but a few of our main items of equipment.

Next morning I set out in high fettle to purchase supplies. John followed me. He seemed to have something on his mind. "What's the trouble, John?" said I. He produced a book on—of all things—*old languages*.

"Do you know the origin of the name Pillaro?" he asked.

"No, and I don't care a damn," I retorted without slackening my pace. That was like John. Having a flair for languages, he was forever delving into the origin of things that had far better be left alone.

But John was persistent. "It means," he said, "The Place of Thieves." Then he ran for his life.

Approaching me later, he asked, "How did it go?" John liked to be right.

"You did them an injustice. The inhabitants didn't ask much more for their stuff than it was worth— at least, not *very* much more—"

John, dismayed, turned to his book.

"—only about two hundred per cent more!"

Everyone was of course convinced that it was only the famous treasure that we sought. The spirit of old Valverde must haunt the place. In truth he should be Pillaro's Patron Saint, for I well believe he has been its principal source of revenue for the last four hundred years. Expedition after expedition has set out from the little place pouring funds, in the form of wages and the purchasing of supplies, into the pockets of its inhabitants. That many have failed before they have gone far does not matter, for a new one comes along. Pillaro should erect a monument to Valverde in its plaza.

Supplies and equipment now being nearly ready, carriers became the next question. What a problem the question of transportation was! As a rule a carrier could be expected to bear a load of from sixty to eighty pounds. But in the difficult country ahead of us that amount was not to be expected, especially as the carriers' own bedding, which they also carry, would have to be heavier because of the rigors of the climate. Moreover, in the high altitudes the peon is accustomed to foods very heavy in weight. It is difficult, if not impossible, to change him to lighter or more concentrated foodstuffs. To insist on it would cause great discontent, and you would in all probability fail to get men at all.

They eat three pounds per day and even on reduced rations, two and a half pounds. A carrier therefore eats up all the food he can carry in from fifteen to twenty days, and then becomes of no use to an expedition.

But the carrier must eat on his return journey also; consequently he can only go forward for from seven to ten days. Add to this the men incapacitated for carrying by adverse travel conditions but who must be fed while in the field and further losses of food by bad weather, accidents, and unavoidable petty pilfering, and it can readily be seen how difficult the problem is.

Forbidding as the Llanganatis are themselves, I am sure it is this matter of commissary that, more than anything else, has caused so many failures and disasters.

This is nearly always the hazard with an expedition that has to travel on foot in a land that is barren of food resources. But it is doubly true in the case of the Llanganatis because of the immense difficulty of the type of travel one faces.

At the time we entered the mountains, scarcely anyone knew anything of the region, and such a thing as a guide was not to be had. Every wrong turn, mistake in the way, or accident of weather would mean delay; and delay meant further dwindling of the precious food supplies, an early return, and failure.

Pillaro lies eastwards of Ambato on the western fringe of the Llanganatis Mountains—a pleasant little country town, its origin lost in a distant past long before the coming of the Spaniards.

Here, some 9,000 feet up, all of us went off our feed, for we were getting into the more rarefied air of the mountains, a great change from what we had recently been through.

It was from here that we hoped to locate the pass through the terrific obstacle of the Llanganatis Mountains to the Oriente. In the whole of Ecuador there are but two trails that lead from its economic centers to that eastern region. Both of these are widely separated by the Llanganatis and adjacent groups forming two arms of a great semicircle which meet, on the other side of the mountains, at Napo. This causes detours involving the loss of many days of travel. It was our purpose to cut through the center of this semicircle and locate a direct route to Napo and the Curaray which could, when opened up, make it possible to accomplish the journey in little more than a day.

Unbelievable as it may seem, the distance is less than eighty miles, the first forty-five miles of which lead over the high barren paramo-lands at an average altitude of from 10,000 to 12,000 feet. These extend to the eastern rim of the cordillera which marks the commencement of the timberline once more and drops away rapidly to the low jungle country of the Oriente.

Once Pillaro is left behind, the whole region is completely uninhabited. Even game is very scarce, until the small settlement of Napo, on the first edge of the Oriente, is reached.

The high, bleak paramo-lands, broken up amidst the gigantic peaks of the Andes, are great expanses of prairies covered by long wiry grass and weeds interspersed with numerous wild morasses and bottomless swamps. On the eastern slopes below these paramos, at about 10,000 feet, the forest country begins and stretches downward to meet the jungle vegetation of the Amazon basin, at about 5,000 feet.

This intermediate area of forest country (called *montaña*) is a region of terrific wooded declivities cut through by torrential cascades and mountain streams which fall precipitously to swell the headwaters of the Amazon. The borderlines of the paramos and these dismal forests, continually enshrouded in mist, are the habitat of the rare and seldom-seen hairy tapir and spectacled bear, which are unique to this region.

Much of the area to be explored and mapped would include the territory covered by Valverde's historic Guide to the lost mines, and the little town of Pillaro is the last point of civilization before entering the mountains. It is the place whence Valverde started on his journey so long ago, and interest in the old Guide now revived in all of us, especially in Bill Klamroth. He went through it word for word, carefully enumerating the landmarks in the order Valverde indicated them.

First he listed the "Farm of Moya," then "the "Guapa," then "flechas," then "sangurimas," and next "the forest." All seemed fairly clear as far as the "Mountains of Margasitas" [pyrites].

"After passing the Margasitas the directions in the Guide seem involved," said Bill.

"Yes," I replied, "the end of the Guide is extremely vague and of little help; and it does not even state definitely where the vast treasure is to be found. For, while it implies that it is within a *socabon*, or tunnel, yet the searcher is directed to the 'third mountain' and is informed that, providing the Guide is correctly interpreted, 'the waters of the lake fall into the tunnel.'"

"Neither does Valverde mention whether the treasure is to be found in the form of golden vessels, utensils, ingots, or a mine or deposit of virgin gold," he broke in.

"Indications are, however," I continued, "that they are ancient gold workings; for he refers to a 'furnace' that is 'nailed with golden nails.'"

I had always thought that the fact that the Llanganatis treasure was thrown into a lake has been given undue prominence, possibly through the romantic features attached to the story. It would appear to be of far greater importance to discover the ancient mines from which the gold had been extracted. An invaluable clew to their location would be the discovery of some ancient roadway.

Just at this time I met Señor Quinteros, "old Q," as we called him, whose stories held out a hope of finding what we sought.

Tall, slender, with grizzled gray beard, and forever enfolded in an ancient black swinging poncho cape, old Q might have stepped out of some old-world portrait painted in Spain's heyday. Always courteous in the extreme, he had the true grand manner.

Scarcely had I met him and acknowledged his sweeping bow, than he rambled off on his one great dream—Valverde and the Treasure. His life was completely wrapped up in it. He knew the old Guide by heart, every version of it, and was convinced he knew where other seekers had gone wrong. Dwelling here in Pillaro, in the very shadow of those great peaks and amid mangled copies of worn old maps, penciled sketches, and diagrams, he had spent his life trying to solve the Valverde riddle.

He spent hours in my company, not by my choosing but his. Desperately anxious to join us, begging to be taken, he asked for nothing more in return than "anything I chose" to give him should we be successful in finding the "Lost Mines." But I had already decided to take him—for quite a different reason.

During his rambling talks of previous trips into the mountains, and he had made several, he talked constantly of a "mountain crowned with gold" with a straight row of palm trees at its base.

To the devil with his "mountain of gold"! I didn't believe a word of that, but the "straight row of palm trees"—*straight*—that was something. If true it meant the hand of man had been there before!

The existence of palm trees on the eastern slopes of the Llanganatis was by no means beyond the realm of possibility. The more sheltered valleys on that side, on the equator as they are, drop rapidly to the low altitudes of the Oriente, and tropical foliage could be expected.

If old Q's palm trees existed and were in a "straight line," it was reasonable to suppose they had been artificially planted at some time or other. This might mean an ancient roadway, and a road might lead to anything! People don't build roads for no reason. Where could one such lead to? I wondered. Old frontier posts of the Inca Empire? Or old mines? To find such a road might lead to a discovery that would save months of indiscriminate search based on old maps, old guides, and the like. In fact, during all my explorations in the Llanganatis I was constantly on the lookout for signs of an old roadway as a first clew, far more than any "Three Peaks," lakes, or cascades.

That there were such mines and such hoards of accumulated gold is unquestionable. When the captive Atahualpa, imprisoned in a room in Cajamarca, sought to buy his freedom and his life by promising the Spaniards to fill that room with gold "as high as he could reach," he commanded that great stores of raw gold, as well as gold and silver articles, should be brought from the distant mines of his empire. We know that a great quantity did arrive.

It is said that at the time Atahualpa was put to death there were numbers of carriers, each bearing a load of seventy-five pounds of gold, en route from the Chuquis district to Cajamarca to swell Atahualpa's ransom. When word of his death was received, this stupendous treasure was concealed in a pit or cave near Piscocamba, and has never been found.

The same thing happened to many other treasure trains, of which the Llanganatis treasure was presumably one. Concealed in pits, caves, lakes, and so forth, in inaccessible and secluded districts of the Andes, many of them, and the mines from which they came, never have come to light.

What fascination those long-departed Incas and their treasures have held for generation after generation of men! My mind turned to the beautiful legend of their origin—the Children of the Sun. The story was that the great Sun God, looking down, saw the miseries of humanity; whereupon he chose his favored son, the Inca, to descend to earth and spread a gospel of abundance for all.

And the legend became history; for it was the Inca race's destiny to spread throughout the Andean regions and convert a disordered mass of barbarians into a magnificent empire with the finest social system that the world has ever recorded.

Innumerable granaries and shelters made travel secure over a vast network of roads which interlaced the empire; with this went a communication system capable of sending messages 150 miles in a day. Magnificent buildings, textiles, and featherwork that led the world of their period, missionaries who taught by example of their far finer husbandry and intelligent mode of life rather than by a pedantic formula— this was the Inca Empire.

Gold and precious stones were abundant. They speak of their temples standing amidst gardens filled with trees, birds, fountains, and flowers—all made of gold and precious stones.

Yet to them gold was an ornamental, almost mystic, thing, durable, easily worked, and beautifully symoblic of the sun. Nowhere else in the world was it considered in such a light.

The Incas, whose existence was unknown outside South America, lived happily, contentedly, free from avarice or ambition and their torments. No one was rich; and no one was poor; yet they possessed wellnigh as much gold as all the rest of the then-known world.

Then Spain came, like all white nations of her time, lured on to new conquests and atrocities by the tales of Inca gold; and within three short years a contented empire of nearly twenty million souls was conquered, enslaved, and utterly destroyed.

The Spanish conquest of the Incas, with its astounding mixture of unparalleled cruelty and indescribable bravery, is an incredible page of history.

But what fearful vengeance was to follow in the course of the Incas' gold, for even before the accumulated treasures had left the land, the Dons were fighting among themselves. Before the Empire had been drained of its golden hoards, nearly every leader of the Spanish Conquest had died at the hands of his own countrymen, fighting for possession of the treasure.

Blood and battle accompanied the loot to Panama. Attracted by the gold-laden galleons, the buccaneers and pirates scuttled the Spanish ships, murdered and tortured the Dons, and sacked their towns.

The gold reached Spain and armies fought for it, sailors voyaged for it, and millions toiled for it. Down through the ages it has spread, like a contagious pestilence, to become the ultimate lure and final goal for which we give our very lives—The Gold Standard of the World!

Chapter XIII
TOWARD THE TREASURE

On March 31, 1936, we set off up the mountain, accompanied for a short distance by the peons' women. On saying good-by they waved, shouted, and wished us "freedom from disaster."

The leave-taking was impressive, taking place as it did in the open country outside the town where the blue vistas of Ecuador seemed almost like a specially designed backdrop for our little drama.

Glancing back as we got under way, I saw a sight to thrill the heart of any man on the march. The men came after me in single file, a long wavering ribbon of brown, bulking shapes—lanky, long-striding Bill Klamroth, looking back frequently to see that the peons were keeping up, the smaller George with an eye to the commissary, and John Ohman as rear guard and watcher for possible stragglers. And somewhere in the line, but more frequently under my feet, was Napo, exuberant and obviously happy to be out of the confines of Pillaro and on the move once again.

During the first morning old Q babbled incessantly of his "mountains crowned with gold." I was anxious to ask him more about those palm trees, but I feared any undue interest in them might influence his answers. It was a steady climb, which the peons took very leisurely, excusing themselves by pleading that "this is the first day." (Later I was to discover that every day was a "first day.")

The veil of superstition in which the whole region of the Llanganatis is cloaked had not affected us while we were in Pillaro, but it was to become apparent later on, as we entered the eerie land ahead of us.

Many people even today think there are Indians throughout the whole Inca Empire who know the exact location of these lost treasures and pass the information from father to son on oath that it shall never be divulged. To do so, they claim, is to invoke the curses of their forefathers upon them. In some books containing information given by the old priests shortly after the conquest, one finds the belief mentioned that the Incas or their descendants will never disclose the whereabouts of these treasures except to a man "of good heart." This worthy is further warned not to use what he finds to the detriment of the natives, but rather to employ it to their betterment.

It is quite possible that in the secrecy of their hearts some Indians know where hidden treasures lie but will never admit it, for behind their secrecy lie unspeakable atrocities committed against their forebears by the Spanish conquerors.

In the afternoon rain came on, and what a different rain it was from the warm downpours of the Oriente! Biting, cold, and in continuous blasts, it penetrated to the bone. Believe me, as it fell without let-up, I had a longing for the once-bemoaned heat of the Curaray basin. But our spirits were high; for before us lay the final, and in many respects the most important, territory to be explored and in it hopes of Inca gold!

Here in the Llanganatis the trade winds, sweeping countless miles from the east across the lowlands of the Amazon Valley, strike the great barrier of the Andes only to be forced abruptly upwards to great heights, where they condense into immense banks of gargantuan, weeping clouds.

If there is any choice of a good season it would be October to December. Yet here we were in our world of perpetual mists and biting, never-ceasing rains with the worst, the snow months, just ahead.

By the afternoon we had reached the spot where the farm of Moya once stood, an open flattish slope covered by knee-high grass and a few stunted trees. Continuing on up the mountain-side, now amid the high open paramo country, we went into camp.

The "Farm of Moya and a short distance above it" —the first landmark mentioned in Valverde's famous Guide! Suddenly the whole story of Valverde's hoard seemed transformed from a mere legend to a vivid actuality. He and his Inca wife must have stood on this selfsame spot centuries before. Laden with gold, they must have passed along this very trail we were following.

There above us stood the second landmark, the "Mountain of Guapa," looming up through the mist against the sky, and by noon on the next day we had reached the "Pongo," or pass, of the Guapa, over which, at an altitude of more than 12,000 feet, a bitter cold wind drove a light rain into our faces.

It was a faint indication of what lay ahead of us, for the rainy season had now set in. The labyrinth of ridges and snow-covered peaks, considered impassable at all times, was now said to be impossible even to enter, let alone to pass through. As we crossed the pass, it was a desolate, forsaken world that spread before us. Amid mist and rain, sleet, and penetrating cold, the peaks reared their ice-sheathed summits fifteen thousand feet into the air.

Even after descending from that inhospitable pass, we were afforded slight protection in the valley, nor did the rain show any sign of abating. By late afternoon it let up somewhat; and arriving at a tiny copse, the only timber thereabouts, we took advantage of its shelter and went into camp for the night.

A short while before sundown the skies cleared, and across the lovely valley lay what was once the *tambo* (shelter) of Mamarita with the lakes of Pisayambu behind it, all shown on Guzman's old map. Off to the northeast the peaks of Roncador stood out like a fortress.

In such localities as the Llanganatis Mountains, tim-

Above: The First Night. "... the farm of Moya, and sleep a good distance above it...." (*No. 1 on Expedition Sketch*)

Below: "... thou wilt see two small lakes called 'Los Anteojos'..." Note the Point of Land Like a Nose and the Heavy Mist in the Background. (*No. 6 on Expedition Sketch*)

Above: Valley Leading to the Treasure Lake of Col. Brooks. Cerro Hermoso, "Sacred Mountain" of the Llanganatis, in Background

Below: The "Three Peaks" above the Treasure Lake of Col. Brooks (*No. 13a on Expedition Sketch*)

bered areas such as the small copse where we were camped are few and far between, but rivers numerous. Here it is timber, rather than water, as in the Oriente, which rules the day's march. This often results in very slow progress. Not infrequently there may be two timbered areas only a few miles apart, with no others for many miles, and thus a day's march may not cover more than two or three miles.

Here Amador, one of our peons, cut the sole of his foot on a rock. Imperturbably he proceeded to sew up the gash with a needle and thread.

After a freezing night we left Mamarita behind and had considerable trouble passing the "wild morass over which thou must cross." A light rain came on once more, but we were still afforded some protection by the great valley in which we traveled. It all seemed strangely familiar; for here again, after struggling through several morasses and as the ground dropped away on crossing a rise, we finally came upon the small twin lakes of Anteojos. There could be no mistake about them. Between them is a point of land like a nose that gives the lakes an appearance for all the world like a pair of spectacles.

So small they were that we could easily have missed them. We stood motionless on a small rise, four strange-looking figures heavily muffled in our sheepskins of brown and white, gazing down over the two sheets of water, each one of us lost in thought.

Here Valverde had left his horses, unable to take them farther. Here also, a few years later, had passed the ill-fated expedition of the King of Spain. What a motley throng! Spanish soldiers with their clanking armor, priests with flowing robes, pushing onwards through swamp, morass, and river, looking eastwards eagerly, ever hopeful of finding Valverde's cache.

We continued on in the same direction; and, though hindered by swamps, we were afforded more protection from the weather by the narrowing of this great valley. Ascending an abrupt rise, we looked down to see Yana Cocha, the "Great Black Lake, the which leave on thy left hand." Its distance from the Anteojos was a pleasant surprise, for it turned out to be a far shorter distance than the impression given by the curious old Guzman map. Guzman certainly must have covered a tremendous amount of ground in this region, a very wonderful achievement under the conditions of his day, but the map that today is attributed to him is drawn on pictorial lines that give no accurate sense of distance or even, in many parts, of direction.

The immense difficulties under which our own sketching and mapping were now being carried out made us realize how much easier it would be just to remember the country and draw a nice little picture of it afterwards amid the comforts of civilization, as was done in the case of some old maps. The constant bad weather made the chances for "long shots" to get our bearings few sand far between; and the making and preservation of records in that chill, watery climate, without shelter for pencil or paper, was no little effort.

While fighting one's way on foot, charting the interminable maze of mountains, I thought that here even the high efficiency of modern aerial photographic mapping would be baffled. Dependent upon the caprices of those massive banks of clouds, a flyer might suffer delay after delay, perhaps for months, until a break in the dense atmosphere would happen to lay bare, for a few moments, the labyrinth below.

From here Bill and I, taking with us old Q and some peons, explored and mapped the region to the southeast. It was in this direction, old Q assured us, that his "line of palm trees" lay. This was rather south of the line which I personally believed Valverde's Guide indicated, but nevertheless previous seekers after the treasure have always followed this southerly course. In any case, at that time, our best chances of finding a west to east pass through the mountains appeared to be in that direction.

We arrived at a sharp, precipitous drop where we "descended along the hillside" to reach a "deep ravine." Crossing this successfully, we continued our steep descent. By now we had dropped down out of the barren, icy regions above the timber line and, circling a bluff on our right, we saw before us the edge of Valverde's next landmark — "the forest." We plunged in. Dark, dank, and drear, every leaf and hanging strand of moss dripped ceaselessly with moisture from the incessant rains. Not even the hearts of

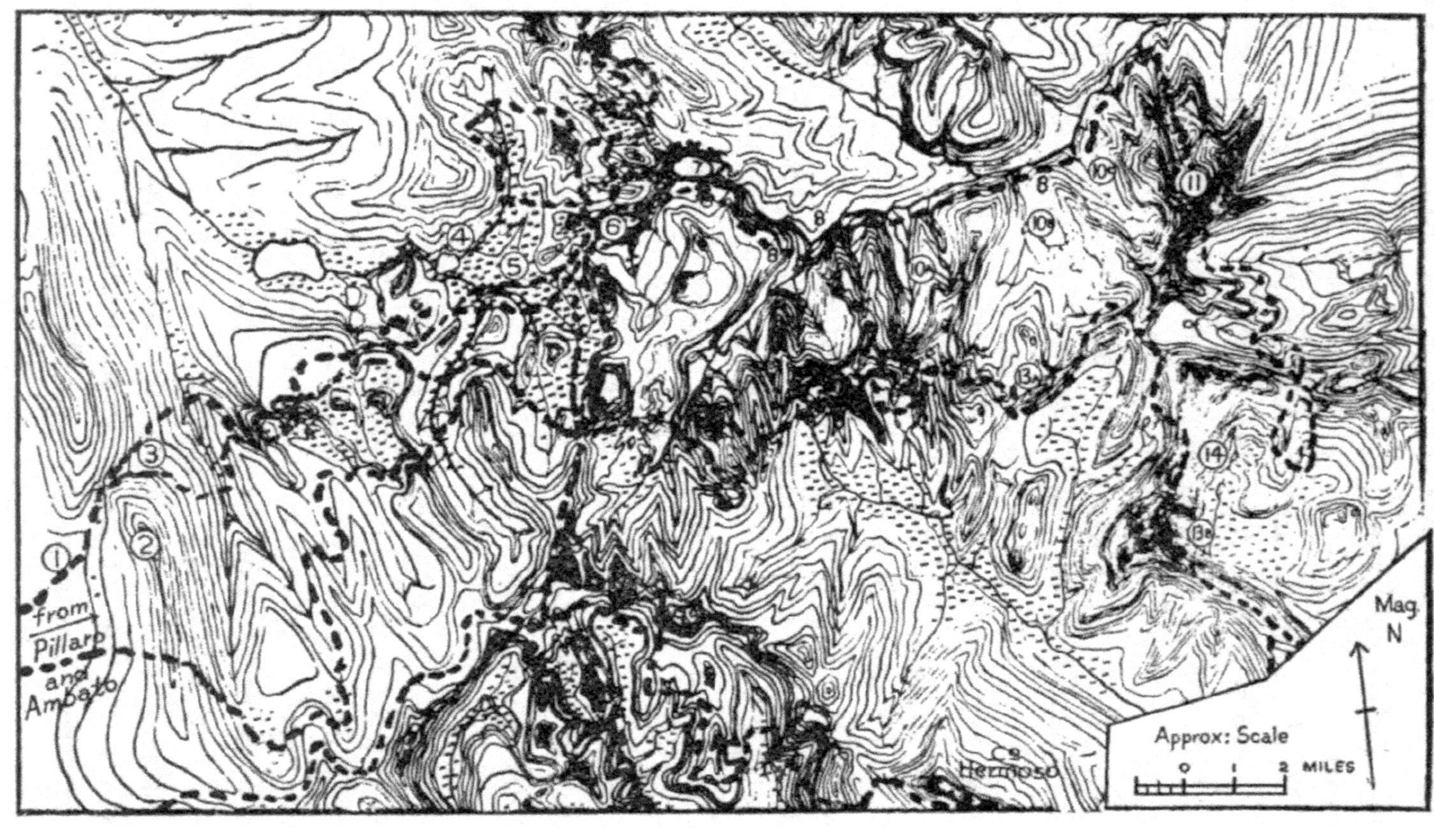

from Pillaro and Ambato
Hermoso
Mag. N
Approx: Scale
0   1   2 MILES

KEY *to fragment of Expedition sketch of Llanganatis, showing where previous searches have been
made.*

- - - - Portion of Expedition's itinerary.

1. Old site of Moya Farm.

2. Cerro Guapa.

3. Pongo (pass) de Guapa.

4. Old site of Mamarita cattle corral.

5. "Wild Morass."

6. Twin lakes of "Los Anteojos."

7. The "great black lake."

8. The "forest."

9. The first ravine.

10-a-b-c. Ravines.

11. Valley deathtrap and fateful pass.

12. "Old Q's" valley of the mountain "crowned with gold."

13-a. Colonel Brook's "Three Peaks and Treasure Lake."

13-b. A perfect "three peaks" in the form of a triangle, with
      lake. But other stipulations are wanting.

14. Signs of what appears to be an ancient roadway.

large fallen trees were dry enough to afford fuel for our campfires. We spent days cutting our way through this ghostly world of chill, depressing misery.

Finally we commenced to ascend, and as we emerged from the edge of the forest once more, we came in sight of a possible "Margasitas" mountain, the stumbling block of so many searchers for the treasure. We had hoped to pass this and reach a "grass valley" beyond, but the rain had been unceasing the whole day, and the men became utterly exhausted with climbing the wet and slippery mountain. To add to this, Bill cut his leg badly with his machete while clearing the trail, and so we went into camp perched on the mountain-side.

It was a miserably cold, rainy night; there was no space to pitch our tents. We were thankful for dawn and a chance to be doing something other than shiver and curse. We tried to find consolation in the thought that a few hours more would find us in a "grass valley" beyond. But we were over-optimistic. We spent the whole of the next day, amid downpours of rain, striving to find a passable route across the mountain's spur. The country commenced to get more difficult. This way certainly gave no indications of a good route through to the Oriente.

On the following day we took a somewhat lower line, and after many hours of laborious climbing reached the lip of a small sheltered valley set high up in the mountain. We were now some 10,000 feet up, and the two days' delay on that false "Margasitas" had been a severe drain on our provisions.

The valley wherein we now pitched camp was almost fantastic. In appearance a small grassy oval, perhaps six hundred yards in length by four hundred in width, it was entirely surrounded by towering mountain peaks except for a narrow cleft on one side where a stream which passed through the center of the valley flowed between the rocky walls to a lip and formed a cascade to plunge several hundred feet to the river below.

As we entered, the sun chose to make one of its rare appearances. Bees, butterflies, and birds flitted about; and the sudden change from the dismal rain-swept mountains and bitter cold revived everyone's spirits. Lovely as the spot was, it would become a potential death trap in the event of a cloudburst such as Colonel Brooks met, upon the surrounding mountains.

Near the lip was the highest ground in the valley, with a solitary tree growing on it. Bill and I picked one slight rise; old Q and the peons another; all were soon in camp and in our sleeping bags.

I slept peacefully until midnight, when I was awakened with a start. Someone was calling. Rain drummed heavily on the tent top as I strained my ears to listen. It was Bill.

"Is there any water in your tent?"

That seemed an odd question; we had been living in water for the past few weeks. But almost before I could answer, the whole canvas bottom of my tent gave an upward lurch, and rose some four or five inches off the ground.

I leaped up to find a foot or more of water pouring in, short-circuiting my flashlight, which was on the floor beside my bed. Grabbing up instruments and precious records, I hastily threw them into a haversack and floundered out into the coal-black night, only to be met by a freezing deluge which had already buried the valley floor waist-deep in water.

I remembered the solitary tree, the only one in the vicinity; and, struggling and wading, I reached it and lashed the haversack high up in the branches. Here I was joined by Bill, and as the flood was gaining every moment and the rain still coming down in torrents, we scrambled up into a fork to spend what was probably one of the coldest nights of our lives.

The men and old Q were on a knoll further away from the main rush, but in the pitch dark, with arms full of records and instruments, it was impossible for us, in the dark, to cross the now raging torrent and reach it. Within fifteen minutes the water had reached the top of the tent doors. We thanked our stars for that lone tree, whose solitary grandeur had impressed itself on our memories so strongly that even in the darkness we could find it.

The pitch-black night in the treetop seemed never to end for Bill and myself. The branches in which we were perched were coated with six inches of sopping wet moss. The rain was descending in torrents;

and, soaked to the skin and chilled to the bone, we were unable to move sufficiently even to keep warm.

The real risk was falling asleep, tumbling out and being carried over the now appalling cascade. We used every artifice to keep each other awake.

We were assisted in this by a last-minute thought I had had of bringing along our emergency bottle of whisky. This, I assured Bill, was to be used for medicinal purposes only. He acquiesced, and soon an empty bottle plopped into the torrent below to go on the long, long journey to the Amazon and thence to the distant Atlantic Ocean.

If I had ever had any doubts about the story of Colonel Brooks' being flooded out of his Treasure Lake by a cloudburst, they were quickly dispelled.

As a dismal dawn finally broke upon us through the mist, we descended to a flooded camp. Rain fell for two days and two nights thereafter; and, when the sun finally shone through and the waters had receded, we found that most of our precious food supplies, which had not been in sealed cans, had perished.

The loss of our food supplies made a great difference in our plans for the future, and we waited impatiently for a break in the weather; but the rain continued for several days, and our already sodden bedding had no chance to dry out—rather, we found signs that it was beginning to rot, a great hardship and cause of suffering even at this altitude; and ahead of us were the lofty peaks of the Llanganatis with their sleet and snow, which would render sleep well-nigh impossible. The peons with us began to show a certain passive resistance and muttered among themselves about going back. The way to circumvent this was to send their food supplies and equipment on ahead of ours, which we proceeded to do. We camped at the end of the day's climb in a freezing fog accompanied by half a gale. We were held in camp by this for two more days.

However, on the third day we got away, and after a morning of slithering in ankle-deep mud and scaling precipitous walls of rock, we made camp at the foot of a gigantic rock mass towering thousands of feet into the air, over which we had to cross.

The next day, April 17th, we headed for a higher pass at the back of the peaks. En route we encountered a tunnel, or *socabon,* beside a small lake, which drew forth a few mutterings from old Q. Nothing developed from our examination of the place, however. It was a natural tunnel—rather a cave with a small outlet at the back—but we found no signs whatsoever of man's handiwork anywhere about, nor any site nearby particularly favorable to catch the prevailing winds. This latter is a significant point, for it was the custom of the Incas to smelt their ores in furnaces placed in natural rock crevices, or chimneys, where, at that altitude, the wind created strong drafts which made a natural bellows for the smelting furnaces. These vertical currents of rushing wind carry with them banks of mist which ascend to great heights. This gives these perilous crags the appearance of being volcanoes pouring forth great clouds of smoke. It was this which caused the belief that the whole region was one of active volcanoes, and hence the continued use of the word *Volcan* in Guzman's map.

The ascent to the pass was laborious in the extreme, for the surface of the mountain was covered with jucal, a long, stiff, cane-like grass growing to a height of some eight feet, which resisted every attempt to get through. In patches it had dried and fallen to the ground in great masses. This presented an even worse obstacle, for the hard shell casing was as slippery as ice and offered no foothold. The only way we finally reached the pass was by finding a tapir trail which, through constant use, had worn a slight passageway to the top.

"Passageway" is only a relative term, for the precipitous and perilous places up which it led would have been difficult to accept as possible had I not seen them for myself.

On many occasions these tapir trails were our salvation. In fact, whenever Bill and I were in doubt as to the easiest way to reach a point or scale a hill, we began looking for a tapir trail, for it had been our experience that we could often better trust to the animals' judgment than to our own. They would fool us sometimes, however, and lead us serenely right to a precipice edge down which they had apparently flitted airily. Then there was nothing for us to do except retrace our steps in search of a safer route. It is almost unbelievable that these heavy four-legged animals can scale the perpendicular places they do.

Sometimes at dawn from the *cuchillo* tops we would hear a sudden outbreak of yelping and howling of wolves down below us. It would last for a short while only and cease as suddenly as it began. (*Cuchillo* tops are fine vantage points from which to watch game, for most wild animals never look upwards.) This howling is usually an indication of the wolves' morning rabbit attack. Rabbits abound in the more sheltered spots of the Llanganatis. Four or five of the wolves surround a swamp where the rabbits come out to feed after dawn. As if at a sudden command, when they have reached their vantage points, the wolves attack from all directions, throwing the rabbits into complete confusion. Each wolf will go after as many rabbits as he can handle, giving each one a quick snap and throwing it into the air. Each wolf is apparently quite confident of his one snap, for he never stops to look, but immediately dashes after the next one without halting his pace. It is at this time that they give out this sudden howling and yelping, which is quite eerie to hear from the distance. It is only when they have killed all the rabbits in sight and the remainder have escaped that they return to collect their bag, apparently never forgetting where they left a dead rabbit in their rush.

Owing to the profusion of rabbits in the paramo regions of the Llanganatis, this is the wolves' common way of getting their food. From our experience, however, I believe that a wolf who grows too old to hunt with this speed takes to marauding at night singly.

One can but be amazed at the marvelous understanding which must pass between a group of wild animals such as these wolves. All at different points, each hidden from the other, how can they know when that instant has arrived for each simultaneously to launch his concerted attack. Who gives the word "go"?

Compare this to a similar evolution with a group of men, even those highly trained for the purpose. They could not hope to compete with such co-operation. Whistles would blow, bugles would blare, and orders rap out. The result?—First one head, then another and another would appear, one after the other, in succession, faltering uncertainly, while the whole maneuver would end in a cloud of dust and blasphemy out of which would emerge the inevitable figure of Private X, without hat or rifle, asking what it was all about!

Bill and I, on ahead of the others, finally reached the top of the pass, a narrow ridge but a few feet across, at an altitude of 12,320 feet. Overshadowed by terrific crags, with a drop of many hundred feet on each side, the perilous knife edge, where the wind whistled with tremendous force, seemed like the world's end, from which we gazed beyond into another realm. At our feet was a precipice down which we peered into the swirling mists below, searching for old Q's next landmark.

Suddenly the shadowy forms of the peons broke through the mist. I turned eagerly to question old Q, but to my surprise an abrupt change had come over him. He became vague in the extreme, and for a man of his natural courtesy, almost surly. He refused to sit near us, and when I asked about his "mountain," he answered that he didn't know, nor even the way.

The thought of spending a night on this inhospitable knife-edge was an unpleasant one, and we were carefully feeling for a way down when the mist thinned for a few moments to show us below a long pear-shaped lake with an outline impossible to mistake—old Q's landmark, as described by him and marked on his map.

Old Q's strange manner there on top of the pass caused me to reflect for a moment on his actions over the past few hours during our ascent to the pass. At first he had been eager to get on to his "mountain of gold," but of late he had hung back and had been of little use in directing our steps. Yet there was no doubt whatsoever about our being on the right line—he had described it far too often. We could get nothing out of him now, however; in fact he would hardly speak, and gave every evidence of having changed his mind, and appeared to be brooding over something.

This became more and more apparent as we climbed down the ridge, heading for a cave under an overhanging rock. Old Q deliberately trailed behind us, making no effort to show us the way.

We pushed on toward the cave, hoping it would afford a warm and sheltered camp.

Progress became easier—until we committed that ever-tempting folly of taking a short-cut. This time it was a pleasant-looking patch of grass down below which lured us. Forsaking the rugged edge of the *cuchillo,* a long, narrow, knife-edged ridge, down which we were slowly working our way, we dropped sharply down to the "green patch."

Before we knew it we were imprisoned, not in grass, but in jucal which ran to a height of some two feet over our heads. To retreat back up the steep ascent was impossible, and it took us two hours and a half to force our way through but a few hundred yards of the obstruction to our cave, where, exhausted, we went into camp just as daylight departed.

But our hopes for a warm shelter here were short-lived, for the shallow cave exuded a dampness that bit into one's bones. The drip, drip, drip of the moisture falling from the roof continued without ceasing.

By the next morning it was raining hard again, but although old Q was a little more tractable, his statements and descriptions became so confusing, involved, and contradictory that they became a menace. He had become a changed man. I tried kindness and threats. I said I would send him back if he did not help us now. Finally he gave in and, setting out, we worked our way to a chain of three lakes threaded together like huge beads upon a slender string of river. Here we climbed up 1200 feet to a narrow pass through which we entered a magnificent valley. Open and pasture-like, and covered with a growth of stiff grass, it was of enormous size. On the east it was bounded by very lofty mountains, barring easy progress in that direction, and on the west and southwest by the spurs of the great range over which we had come. Towards the south it fell away gently, stretching far into the distance until it was lost in an abrupt end where it met the great forested area of the Oriente.

Before leaving that day, old Q had sworn that his "mountain of gold" lay over this pass, at the foot of this enormous valley. This was borne out by his sketch map. But he now became hopelessly vague.

"This is the valley, Señor, this *is* the valley," he mumbled; "but I do not recognize the mountains, and as for my beautiful 'mountain of gold'—I do not see it."

The rugged outline of the mountains surrounding the valley was so outstanding that once seen they could never have been forgotten. Disgusted, I alternately stormed and raved, or was gentle and sympathetic, but to no avail. Our indecision and the unnatural loneliness and solitude of the great valley affected the peons, who commenced to lose confidence. They wailed that we were lost, that we would all perish miserably; and we returned to camp wet, disappointed, and disconsolate.

Our nights spent in the congested space of the damp clammy cave were dismal beyond words, and our food was now reduced to a perpetual diet of lentils—all that remained with us. This finally drove us back over the pass to our reserve dump to replenish.

We soon returned, however, to this forgotten land, but, upon crossing the pass this time, took a higher line towards what appeared to be drier country. By now I had lost hope of Q's line of palm trees, but the next night he came to me and told me that he was about to give me a great confidence: that he now knew where his "mountain of gold" was. It was quite close, he said, and he earnestly wished to take us there in the morning. He was sincere and genuine in his belief, I was convinced; and, having come so far, I determined to give him one more chance on the morrow.

Dawn came, and we awakened to see right before us, breaking through the mist, the pride and majesty of the Llanganatis, the Cerro Hermoso. This giant peak named "Beautiful Mountain" has been vested with sacredness in the old legends. We had long since circled this peak, and were now well to the east of it; but, owing to the constant bad weather, this was the first time we had seen it.

Everyone was soon astir, and we made an early start, old Q ahead and now apparently brisk and eager to show us his great secret. He warmed up to his subject with the old enthusiasm he had had in Pillaro. He talked quite rationally until of a sudden I saw again that strange, far-away look return to his eyes as he murmured something about the great confidence and something that had never before been seen by a white man other than himself. This was his mission, he said, and once it was accomplished he was ready for death.

Such talk would have been enthralling but for that look in his eyes.

His pace became slower and slower. He didn't seem ill, but that moroseness which I had come to recognize quickly was upon him again. He now declared he could not reach the place of the palm trees before nightfall. Then suddenly from behind me I heard a groan, and turning found he had collapsed.

Here was a hellish situation. Bill and the men were on ahead out of sight, and nothing would induce old Q to get up. He lay on the desolate ridge writhing and moaning, refusing to say what ailed him, and with night not many hours away.

Rushing to the rim of the ridge, I yelled at the top of my voice just in time to catch Bill as he went over the crest, far ahead of us. I shouted for him to make camp and send back some men with a tent fly to serve as a litter, then seated myself beside the old fellow to await help.

I pondered deeply on old Q and his dreams. I couldn't make him out. I am sure that he was thoroughly convinced of the truth of his statements about the palm trees and "mountain of gold." He believed them utterly, and it must be remembered that he had not asked me for any money at all and never did, to any extent.

The men finally arrived, but he steadfastly refused to be carried in the tent fly. He wouldn't move from the ground and, fearing internal injuries, I was forced to let him have his way. Erecting a tent over him I left him in the safekeeping of two peons for the night and set off on a now terrible journey back to camp, for darkness had fallen.

No longer able to see sufficiently to pick my way, my only course was to follow a straight line; and that took me through the worst jucal I had yet encountered. Bill sat on a ledge above the camp throwing a beam of his flashlight in an attempt to keep me in the right direction, but the mist which had shut down again made this ineffectual. Forcing my way through the dense growth, tearing my hands and falling into holes and hollows, I finally stumbled into camp about ten o'clock that night.

That was the end of Q as what you might call an active member of the party. When I saw him months afterwards in Pillaro he was perfectly normal. It was only when he crossed that fateful pass that he seemed to come under the influence of those terrific, awe-inspiring, desolate peaks. My opinion is that years of meditating on his great dream of the treasure, mine or gold mountain, had crystallized them for him into actual fact.

I am sure he honestly believed that he had at one time seen them. But, when faced by people who, like ourselves, sought to run the dream down rather than talk about it, his conscious mind was forced against a blank wall.

The time had come when he had either to accept

the brutal realization that his dream was a figment of fancy or to invent some subterfuge to avoid the issue. It was not that he wanted to deceive me, but that he could not face undeceiving himself.

I was very sorry for old Q, for I have known many similar cases of such autosuggestion induced by solitude or brooding.

Making a detour somewhat to the south of the line of our entry, however, with the idea of covering that region also, we came to the lake that popular belief says was the one reached by Colonel E. C. Brooks.

Our reward was an old weather-beaten camp site, presumably his. Near at hand, leading to the edge of the lake, was a long narrow cut, an obvious attempt to drain it at some previous time. Across the water was a strange rock formation which looked for all the world like a replica of a church porch. This expression was used by Valverde in his Guide.

We decided to drag Brooks's lake with a makeshift raft made of jucal grass wrapped in a waterproof sheet. Bill stretched out face downwards on the contraption and paddled his way into the center of the lake, which, fortunately, was not deep.

He used a kerosene can on a rope as a dredge. When the samples had been brought ashore, they were dried off and examined.

Suddenly an interruption! One of the peons jumped into the ice-cold water and commenced to splash about, giggling like a child. But not for joy, for his eyes were staring—the man had gone out of his head.

What the cause was I cannot say. The superstitions surrounding such old treasures in the land of the Incas are indeed extraordinary. That they can be disastrous in the field is evinced by what happened to Colonel Brooks. It will be remembered that his Indian carriers deserted overnight, leaving him to his fate.

Bill's work continued apace. But an examination of the samples disclosed that they contained nothing but *mica*, or "fool's gold." So much for *that* lake.

Chapter XIV
ANIMAL ANTICS

But the search for Valverde's route did not completely monopolize our time and energies. We carried out a constant program of scientific work in which every member of the Expedition assisted, in spite of the never-ending drive to keep the transport going. In this transport work Bill excelled. All the while Ohman kept us in touch with officials in Quito over the radio, which, I'll wager, must have surprised the ether waves of the Llanganatis.

During the course of the Expedition we took every opportunity to collect such natural history specimens as were possible. As is usually the case, this was most satisfactorily done by hunting parties out specially for that purpose and operating within reasonable distance of Pillaro, whither a living specimen could be transported without too great difficulty.

George Brun was ever active in this branch, and in the face of terrible weather conditions carried on some excellent work. Largely through his zeal, we finally succeeded in bringing back to New York over five hundred specimens.

Varied and diverse were the methods we employed to obtain these, for, not being primarily a hunting expedition, and with much difficult work to attempt in other fields, we were not able to carry special traps.

In Ecuador we could learn very little about the "anteojos" bear or the different variations of the species. In some books he is called the "invisible bear," as he is very shy and rarely encountered except at the edge of the timber line of the high paramo country. It is apparently the only species to be found in South America, but we came upon evidences of at least three variations.

There is the small black bear, with no markings, which the Indians call "oso negro." There is a second, apparently larger, type with light tawny markings on his forehead above the nose and between his eyes—"oso frontino." The third and largest has big white circles around his eyes and a white "shirt front." The Indians call him the "anteojos," or spectacle bear.

The belief appears to be that he does not run very large. Yet we brought back two which we did not consider extraordinary when compared with some we had seen and which would have run perhaps four hundred and fifty to five hundred and fifty pounds.

All three types sleep in the woods in the protected ravines and on coming out on the paramo tops are apt to follow the tapir trails, which are clearly marked. Normally the anteojos feeds on a certain cactus which abounds on the paramos and it is his habit to go from one to another, smashing them open with his paw and devouring the inside. Since his table manners are none too delicate, by the time he is through, the white pith has been showered in all directions. A single bear can destroy a great number of cacti at one sitting; and from the distance, if the day be clear, the scene is as if snow had fallen.

The Indians say that when driven by hunger the spectacle bear will descend to the lowland farms and attack a calf or small steer. They contend further that, although shy, when hurt or at close quarters, *ursus ornatus* will face men or dogs fearlessly. Generally speaking, they are extremely difficult to hunt.

The first day we went out for bear, George had extraordinary luck and came upon two feeding together, one of which he declared was considerably larger than the other. In this opinion, it was as big as any black bear he had ever seen, and appeared to be as large as a small grizzly.

George was delighted at the prospect and was stalking them with his men when suddenly a black shape dashed from behind and made for the larger of the two bears. It was Napo, whose courage was to be commended, though his discretion left much to be desired.

Seeing the dog coming, the bear ambled on its way without any increase of pace. It was at this time that George was able to appreciate the immense size of bruin in comparison with Napo, who, though a big dog of some seventy or eighty pounds, looked diminutive in comparison with his quarry.

When Napo came within striking distance, the bear finally deigned to stop and face him. A small white hunting dog belonging to one of the Indians also ran up and got within the bear's reach. The bear shot out a vicious paw, and the little dog flew many feet in the air. He landed completely stunned, and the bear crouched over him. At that moment Napo increased the fury of his attack and diverted the bear's attention, which saved the smaller dog's life.

By this time George and the Indians were close enough to open fire on the smaller of the two bears, which must have been hit in the leg; for some time later, when we obtained our three-hundred-pound specimen, we found a 30-30 bullet implanted in his thigh. Nobody else had been hunting in this region for a year or more, if then; so the bear we later bagged undoubtedly was the smaller of the two which Napo attacked.

He was an old one with worn teeth and from his markings was a "frontino" or second variation of the species. He weighed almost three hundred and fifty pounds. I think the larger one must have been the true "anteojos," and must have run up to five or six hundred pounds in weight.

We made several attempts to capture alive that crowning glory of the Andes—the condor, but failed, largely through lack of time.

The Indians have their own way of catching these

birds, which are very rare and seldom seen. We proceeded to try their method. Selecting a likely spot at about 12,000 feet, we dug a pit, over which we placed a sort of grill of crossed poles lashed together, the whole masked by a grass blind on which we placed a bait of horse meat. Two men then concealed themselves inside the pit and waited for a condor to alight on the grill.

When he does, the idea is that the men should quickly grasp one of his legs, through an aperture left in the roof especially for that purpose, pulling the leg down into the pit and holding on for dear life.

Contrary to common belief, the condor's foot is not a talon that can close on its prey as can the eagle's. It is more like an enormous chicken's foot, unable to grasp anything very tightly.

Pinioned in this awkward position, the condor is unable to use the terrific sledge-hammer blows of his beak against his captors, whom at one stroke he could rip open.

Meanwhile, in another blind at a suitable distance, a second party of men is watching, ready to run out the moment the bird is trapped and lasso the dangerous head. Once this is done the capture is easy.

We tried this for seven or eight days without success. The condors came, but refused to mount the trap; so we tried a different method, that of poisoning the bait with strychnine.

A condor can eat an incredible amount of meat at one sitting but when overloaded finds great difficulty in taking off, especially if there is no ground wind. On such occasions he can be overtaken by a mounted man and lassoed. If surprised in this overloaded state, however, the condor is apt to disgorge the contents of his stomach in order to lessen his weight for the take-off. In his frantic attempts to vomit, he goes through violent convulsions during the course of which his claws strike upward and downward in close proximity to his head. This, I think, accounts for the erroneous belief of the Indians that a condor can "put his claw down his throat to empty his stomach."

But the condor has a phenomenal constitution, for our poisoned meat failed to work, although on one occasion we used as much as three grams of strychnine with no result—enough to kill several men.

They say that if a cat has nine lives, a condor has eighteen, and it certainly appears so; for a bullet through the body seldom brings him down. In fact, on one occasion a condor had practically his whole belly blown out by a 30-30 bullet, yet continued his flight. It is, however, interesting to note that, in the end, the specimen that George did obtain was brought down by a well-directed .22 short.

George and an Indian had located a group near the edge of a ravine. They were mounted at the time, and, as the birds are, apparently, less wary of a horse than of a man on foot, were able to approach to within a relatively short distance. Dismounting and handing his horse over to the Indian, George stalked the birds until he was finally able to arrive at a vantage point. Here he saw a beautiful male with a female close at hand. Resting for a few minutes to recover his breath, a great necessity at that altitude before taking aim, he drew a bead on the male and fired. The whole group immediately disappeared over the edge of the ravine. He ran to the edge just in time to see the female swooping down on the Indian. At the first attack the Indian was able to avoid her blow; and, as she retreated, he fired the contents of a BB shell and hit her. Nothing daunted, the female turned and swooped to attack again. The Indian managed to escape a second time, when fortunately the bird abandoned the attack and continued on her way. George's male condor was found a short distance down the ravine, stone dead with a bullet through its brain.

The bird was a perfect specimen with a wing spread of ten feet eight inches, and is now in the possession of the Academy of Natural Sciences, of Philadelphia.

The male condor is a truly magnificent bird in the air, with a wing spread that I believe sometimes exceeds twelve feet. Jet black all over, except for white tops on the wings that shine like silver in the sunlight, neck bare like the vulture, but encircled by a brilliant snow-white ruff, he is a sight never to be forgotten.

Condors, whether male or female, appear to move their wings very seldom, except when suddenly surprised or because of unusual occurrences. You see them planing in the air by the hour with their enormous wings outspread. In bad weather they avoid the risk of landing on unfamiliar ground, remaining in groups in or about their aeries. These are apt to be in clefts or fissures in the impregnable, wooded cliff faces of the lower and more protected valleys at 10,000 or 11,000 feet. We found such a valley with two groups in it which, as we watched them from a distance, showed no inclination to leave their nesting places until the sun was well up. When the sky was clear, they remained away all day, returning only to sleep.

I believe that the condor must fly, as a rule, at a terrific height; for on those rare clear days you get in the Llanganatis, even while standing at an altitude of 12,000 or more feet, you cannot even see them above you until they decide that all is safe and swoop down on their prey. They circle round and round at a great height, nothing escaping their remarkable vision, and they seem only to risk approaching certain places for their victims on a clear day when they can see from their enormous altitude that all is safe. Sometimes it is only after a considerable period that they come down near the ground, volplaning around a calf or lamb which they have picked as their victim. This they do in numbers of from five to ten. One after another they swoop down on the wretched animal, striking it terrific blows on the head, neck, and back as they pass.

The first two blows usually take out the animal's eyes so that the poor beast is blinded and unable to do anything but stand there helplessly awaiting the successive blows of the other condors. We saw a calf that had been killed in this manner a few minutes before, the condors having been driven off before they could eat it. The eyes were gouged out, the tongue torn to ribbons, and great gashes ripped in its neck and back as if done by a hatchet. A condor, when ripping up the tough hide of dead horses or cattle, will draw back its head and strike downwards with an arching blow of its beak that is like the descent of a scythe.

When one group of condors is approaching a victim another group may also come up. On these occasions the males of each group will sometimes fight. They swoop at each other in the air at a great height, and, meeting with terrific impact, appear to become interlocked and fall like stones for many hundreds of feet, until, presumably on approaching too close to the ground, they break apart again and repeat the performance. They do not appear to duck and circle and flutter about each other as other birds do when fighting.

As the condor often weighs well over sixty pounds (ours weighed that), the force with which they strike each other must be terrific. As they seldom move their wings in the air, they do not give the impression of having such phenomenal speed as they really possess. On one occasion, when through my mapping I happened to know the exact distance to an adjoining ridge, a condor passed quite low over my head. Almost before I could get my camera ready he had reached the other ridge, over two miles away, and yet he didn't look as if he were moving at all.

The Indians say that if the condor is short of his

usual sort of prey, or carrion, he will, if hungry, eat the tops of the small green herbs that grow around the paramos.

Although our strychnine bait failed with the condors, it was quite successful with the smaller hawks, etc., such as the two pairs of rare *curiquingi* which we brought back and which are now in perfect health at the New York Zoo.

While still feeding from the bait on the trap, they appeared unaffected, but as soon as they were rushed and took off to escape, they became dizzy and fell to the ground. By making a small slit in their crops we quickly extracted the poisoned meat; and with the application of medicines they recovered almost immediately.

We made a very different type of capture in the case of an Andean hawk which we had long been anxious to get, dead or alive.

After constant failure we had almost given up hope when a magnificent specimen soared low over our heads with no apparent intention of alighting.

The opportunity was too good for George to miss. He grabbed the nearest weapon, a .22 rifle, and with a lucky shot brought it down.

The bullet had passed cleanly through the middle of the bird's body, but such was its endurance that we saw, to our surprise, that there was a chance of saving its life. After a careful application of antiseptics the wound soon healed. The same night the bird would have eaten, had we permitted it, and within a few days was as well as ever. He is now in Central Park in New York; and, when I last saw him, a year after his capture, he was in as perfect condition as any bird in the zoo.

We had less luck with the tapir, who is nocturnal in his habits. In fact, although we saw quantities of their trails, we only set eyes on two tapir during our whole stay in the mountains.

Taken all in all, the tapir is a pretty odd fellow and may be regarded as among the oldest of living mammals. Whether he appreciates it or not, I have no way of knowing; but according to the scientists he belongs, in company with horses and rhinoceroses, to the small but cliquey family of "odd-toed ungulates."

But the tapir makes trouble over this, for although quite in order with three toes on his hind feet, he disturbs the world of science by having four on his forefeet, which, of course, makes him anything but an odd-toed ungulate in front.

He is a grass eater, usually solitary, shy, and a generally inoffensive fellow, frequenting shady forests in the neighborhood of water. The species that abounds in the low-lying portions of South America is very common and sparsely haired. But there is one unique variety which lives only in the high altitudes around the timber line of the Andes.

This tapir of the high altitudes has white-tipped ears and lips, and grows thick hair up to some two inches or more in length save on his rump. From this latter characteristic the species acquired its name of "hairy tapir." One seen in the distance can easily be mistaken for a bear.

Knowing the rarity of this animal, I had questioned authorities at several museums prior to leaving New York and had found the consensus of opinion to be that he did not normally dwell above 11,000 feet; yet in point of fact we ultimately caught one that must have come over a height of 13,000 or 14,000 feet to reach the place where she became our captive.

At various times during the Expedition we had worked very hard to try to obtain one of these, dead or alive, but to no avail. We went far afield after them and took a great deal of pains to obtain a specimen, but, as time went on, we had to concentrate on our other more important objectives and abandoned all hope of getting one.

However, as so often happens in these cases, we finally got our specimen, alive, when we least expected to. It actually occurred right at the end of the Expedition when I had sent Bill Klamroth on to a point only four hours from Pillaro to obtain a few geographic observations that I still lacked for the completion of our map.

He had just reached this point and was on ahead of his peons when one of them ran up to him and asked for the use of his carbine. Bill asked him why, and he said they had caught a "danta" (tapir). Being then at over 12,000 feet, Bill knew it must be one of these priceless hairy tapirs which, of course, to the peons was nothing more than food.

Bill raced down the mountain-side to find that the peons had lassoed a genuine hairy tapir that had turned at bay in a swamp, which is their custom when chased. Knowing Indians as I do and the methods they have of killing big game by strangulation if they haven't got a firearm, I am sure that they had already attempted to strangle it for food, for although with infinite care Bill managed to get her into Ambato, she refused to eat and died within four days, and upon dissection was found to have a broken blood vessel in her throat. She was rather large to survive the first, always trying, days of captivity, however, being over three hundred pounds in weight even then.

Among other victims of our strychnine experiments was, of course, Napo, George's dog, who would eat anything—including poisoned meat. He must have had the constitution of a condor, however, for, although he did get convulsions once, after taking a little medicine he recovered immediately, and looked around eagerly for more dinner.

Napo was a huge dog of great strength and courage. Utterly fearless in the chase, he would take on a bear single-handed and without pausing in his stride. As gentle as a lamb at other times, he was our constant companion throughout the entire Expedition. Rain or shine, in jungles or on snow-capped peaks, he never missed a day, and is now back in New York City leading a sheltered life of ease, the horrors of the Llanganatis long forgotten.

Once while hunting George was caught in a hail

storm. He started to head back to camp, but, blinded by the hail, he missed his way. Suddenly Napo refused to follow him any farther, turning and going off on his own. It was now George who had to follow the dog; and sure enough Napo's instinct was right. In a short while he brought his master safely into camp.

Napo had little tolerance for situations beyond his understanding. On one occasion two tins of gasoline stored in the hunting shelter blew up, taking the shelter with them. This was too much for Napo, and without further ado he made a bee-line across the paramos, his tail between his legs. He was followed by all the Indian hunting dogs, of which he was now the leader; and the party never drew up until within the shadow of distant Pillaro.

Napo had one blind spot, however. He could never understand that when a man is sleeping at dawn, dreaming of being no longer in the Llanganatis, to burst into his tent, let in the snow, and pounce on his chest with the impact of a small horse—is not the way to say good morning.

I broached the subject to George several times, but he always took Napo's part. He pointed out that this was the invariable custom of French dogs. That closed the whole matter.

Napo had a great time with the rabbits and had the same trick as the wolves of giving a rabbit one snap and a toss in the air; but the rascal would stop to eat his first rabbit and not go after a second one like the wolves. A small one he would eat whole, disgorging the fur afterwards like a vulture. Napo chased after adult wolves once or twice, and it always seemed to be a neck and neck finish. The wolf had the habit of "jinking" from side to side as he ran; whereas Napo, if it was open country, would make a bee-line for him. But once Napo had closed up on the wolf, the latter apparently ceased to think it was funny and put on extra speed. Napo never seemed to get closer than a few feet, and on account of the altitude he soon got winded and had to lie down gasping while the wolf scuttled off.

The young wolves, however, are not so fast, and by chance may be surprised at close quarters. It is then that the hunting dogs can corner them, as the wolves are petrified with fear and remain motionless.

We never succeeded in catching an adult wolf; and, according to the Indians, it would in any case have availed us nothing; for it is said that once in captivity they "never cease to fight, their eyes full of blood, mouths full of foam, and they die of *rage* the same night."

There is controversy as to the identity of these animals, which appear to have certain characteristics of both wolves and foxes. They have unusually long fangs, never seem to become tame, in fact become less so in captivity as they grow older, and, according to Schultz, the zoologist, are more savage than the wolf and more destructive than the fox. They don't appear to be particularly afraid of human beings and have to be most carefully handled in captivity, even when being fed. However, the wolf seems to have great respect for the Indian hunting dogs, and when cornered will cower motionless. At this moment the dogs will, as a rule, not charge but merely hold him at bay. But at the slightest movement on the part of the quarry they will leap on him. He can be caught at this time by throwing a poncho or heavy sacking over him. That is how we captured our three.

The younger ones survive captivity but appear to get less and less tame as they grow older. While one of our men was feeding a captured wolf after it had been in captivity a few weeks, the beast suddenly leaped upon his back and grabbed him between the shoulders. Fortunately the man had on a thick jacket out of which he was able to slip, leaving the wolf to chew it up instead of the back of his neck. They are apparently apt to turn upon one another if placed together. Whether this is only when they are famished or because of the eternal sex business, I do not know; but I recall a case where three were in one cage together, and one morning the owner came to find only two and remains of the third. Nevertheless, he left the two together and returned a second morning to find only one and the fur of the second. I think it quite possible that they were inadequately fed at the time.

For the first few weeks ours would rarely feed if we were present. In fact they were equally vicious whether we were bringing food or not.

They are the very devil to keep in captivity after

you get them. They have the ability of a Houdini to escape. One of our three was temporarily chained to a post in an enclosed cellar. At midnight the man and his wife who were looking after the animals were awakened by a sudden barking of the two watch-dogs in the yard. The noise abruptly ceased, and they paid no more attention.

However, at daylight, when they went into the yard they saw the astonishing tableau of the wolf quite free in one corner and the two dogs, Napo and Mitzi, within six feet of it, all three absolutely motionless and gazing intently at one another. They had apparently been in this posture for over six hours.

After the wolf was recaptured, we found that he had broken loose from his chain, burrowed down through the floor of the cellar underneath its foundations and out on the other side, evidently between sunset and midnight.

When we were entraining the animals and baggage at Ambato for New York, George went to feed one of the creatures which was chained to a post pending being crated. When chained like this, the wolf had the custom of pacing incessantly from side to side, at each turn giving the chain a jerk. This constant jerking had apparently weakened it, for the wolf gave a sudden jump at George and broke the chain.

The animal appeared completely baffled by its sudden state of freedom or didn't realize that it was free, for it continued to swing itself from side to side in the same manner as before. George was alone at the time and single-handed could not recapture the wolf, which could have escaped over the wall quite easily. George went at once to the railway station to get the help of John Ohman and the dogs, who returned with him. This took some half an hour, and, when they got back to the yard, the wolf was still swinging from side to side as if chained to the post, though he could have run away at any moment had he so desired. If there ever was a case of habit persistence this was it.

Two of the wolves were taken safely to New York, where they now are in the Bronx Zoo, with the announcement on their placard that this species is being exhibited for the first time in the United States. No doubt they now fight savagely between themselves over a visitor's peanut.

There was, however, a third escape, which ended very expensively for the Expedition.

In some manner our largest wolf, a female, escaped from her chain in a way that I was never able to discover. It seemed a miracle.

For a while she stayed about on the low housetops and garden walls of Ambato, keeping very quiet in the daytime. But at night she must have realized that she was a lone wolf hunting, and she found it very, very easy. The first we heard of it was a wail and moan from a man who came with one hand out for money and the other full of feathers and chicken legs, which the wolf had fancied the night before. We paid him munificently to hush him up.

The next day it was a woman with even more

chicken legs and feathers—well, as we were still en-
joying the joke then, we paid her, too.

But when it came to a pig that genuinely enough
had been killed—apparently by a savage bite in the
throat—the thing began to get expensive, and we
couldn't keep it quiet any longer.

We set a baited trap for the wolf. She took the bait
but got out of the trap. But with the brilliance of
forethought which running an expedition in South
America gives one, we lied like troopers and told the
populace that we had caught her again. But the very
next night we saw her on top of a wall by the rays of
our flashlights, the collar still around her neck. She
was having a perfectly grand time going from chicken
yard to chicken yard.

By this time the population of Ambato, including
both the army and the police, had abandoned their
routine life to hunt the wolf, but with no success.
Bills poured in on us from every direction. They had
got tired of billing us for chickens and pigs, and they
soon graduated to higher stuff. One man whose horse
had died of old age a considerable time before all this
put in a price that would have bought a very good
race horse, and so on and so forth.

Through the mayor they put in an official com-
plaint to the Police, and the Police most wisely said,
"Caramba! shoot the damn wolf." Well, of course,
that settled the matter, for nobody could, and our
wolf had a grand time for about six weeks. Then we
heard no more of her; so I imagine she found her way
back to the mountains.

Chapter XV

BARRIERS OF A LOST WORLD

DURING the earlier stages of the expedition into the mountains the peons did fairly well. To be sure they had taken their time, always anxious to camp long before the end of the day, and delaying the start in the mornings by their leisurely manner of cooking and eating their breakfasts. But they had not grumbled and had given no trouble.

However, as time went by, their enthusiasm for the enterprise waned in the face of the difficulties and terrific weather. As I recall it, we had thirty-nine days and nights of almost incessant rain. At times the weather became even worse—the rain turned to snow.

A small taste of this was enough for Luis, the cook, who, while back on the convoy, decamped. This was bad news, for although his loss was of minor importance in itself, his idea of running away would soon spread in spite of all precautions. And so it did. The men could be controlled while actually with the main party, but they had to be sent back on supply convoys, and during these periods it was touch and go, although we exerted all possible vigilance.

On one occasion, at dawn, on going to the place where the men had spent the night, not a sound was to be heard. The whole party had vanished, taking with them the load ropes and specially made packs.

I pulled out then and on a rapid trip to Quito obtained an interview with President Paez. The Government of Ecuador was to gain very materially by our mapping and study of this hitherto uncharted area. Being keenly aware of all this, President Paez lent a ready ear and offered to call for volunteers from the army. I shall be eternally grateful to him for the speed with which he carried this out. Within thirty-six hours I had an officer and seventeen men from the engineering corps; with these, and a new batch of Indians and half-breeds, we made a fresh start.

To obviate the extreme loss of efficiency with human transport, I determined to try animals this time for the first stages and form a main supply camp at the farthest forward point we could take them. We hoped that with a certain amount of temporary road-making we could get them past the swamps and morasses as far as the more difficult mountain terrain. The value of these animals was due to the fact that they could be fed on the paramo grass and would not, therefore, consume the loads they carried.

I have found from experience that what is wanted above all things in a saddle or pack horse for work of this sort is endurance and a good walk. The trot and canter on which the natives base their sales talk are a snare and a delusion. I think I set a new fashion in horse dealing in Pillaro, where I purchased our animals, by always trying out a prospective purchase at the walk. As a rule they are galloped off in every direction with a tremendous flourish of tail, hoofs, and dust, which doesn't mean a thing. When the owners saw me trying out a new prospect at a smart walk and disappear for several hours, they were dumb-founded; and for a few days I made some quite good buys. But the canny dealers soon thought of a way that defeated my ends. Every horse in the whole province that could walk, but would drop dead if put to a trot, was brought to me. After much grief on both sides, we compromised.

By June 12th we were again on the familiar trail to the Farm of Moya, Guapa, and the Anteojos, pushing on into that land of false lures and dashed hopes.

Getting them over the numerous swamps was a problem which occupied everybody's efforts, and here Bill Klamroth did fine work. These swamps are really a series of tufts thrusting out of pools of deep mud. A man could cope with them by stepping carefully from one tuft to another. But, with the horses, they became a real difficulty. Across the more extensive swamps we had actually to make roadways. Timber not being available at that high altitude, it was necessary to construct improvised corduroy roads out of the stiff cane grass (jucal). This took a lot of time, and wherever possible in the narrower crossings we would use a very simple device which we called quite affectionately our "wedding carpet." It was a long roll of stiff sacking some four feet broad. We would unroll and spread it across a narrow stretch of swamp, and the problem was solved. As the transport animals have a habit of following each other in single file, we would attempt to rush them across at a smart speed in order to get all of them over before the "carpet" sank down.

The ever-increasing rains soon converted even the higher country into an almost impregnable barrier. Do what we might, it was impossible to prevent the transport animals from getting bogged. The unfortunate beasts would wallow up to their middles, when panic would take possession of them; and, plunging frantically, they would sink deeper and deeper into the mire. Meanwhile the loads would have been scattered to the four winds. Then the problem was to save not only them but also the equipment. It required quick work to extricate the animals, and by the time we reached *terra firma* they were too exhausted to do anything but lie down. The same was true of the men themselves after their desperate efforts. I doubt if ever before any swamps on the entire continent heard such fervent cursing as we gave off during those days.

By keeping at it, however, we made some progress and reached the stream that, according to Richard Spruce, the botanist, is the one which played a prominent part in the King of Spain's first expedition to solve the riddle. For here it was that the priest accompanying the expedition, Padre Longo, whose presence was relied upon to give moral and religious courage to the party, completely disappeared. Apparently no trace of him was ever found, nor has any explanation of his vanishing been advanced. The superstitions of the day were enough, and almost immediately the expedition broke up without going further. As late as the middle of the last century, when Spruce spent considerable time studying the whole matter of the Valverde Guide and treasure, a cross of wood was said by him to be standing by this river. It seems incredible after so long a time, although in the high altitude the cross would be less likely to rot away than in a low-lying area.

Meanwhile, we were proceeding higher and higher, our tent floors almost constantly immersed in water. Both the men and the animals had to be kept moving or they would soon crack. The rain now turned to snow, and the swollen rivers made such fords as had existed earlier impassable. The effort of bringing timber for the bridges from the distant valleys became more and more difficult until we reached the point where even this was impossible.

This was as far as we could use the animals, and when we pushed on we had to change to man power to carry our loads. Not only were the horses suffering, but also such a high proportion of the men that it became evident many would soon have to be sent back.

At this point Valverde's Guide commenced to grow vague. It gave landmarks of a nature that could be found in different places a dozen times a day. A "dry quebrada!" Why, the region was nothing else but— except that they are not *dry*, at least at the season we were there, and Valverde did not say what time of the year he traveled in.

Similarly, his earlier references to "flechas," "sangurimas," and "forest," are little help, for after four hundred years nature's work can make great changes. Lakes with "cascades" abounded, and very logically so. A breakaway, forming a bowl high up in the sides of these mountains, is a common occurrence. The flow of water into the bowl very naturally forms a lake, the only outlet to which is the narrow lip from which height the outflow pours in a cascade many hundreds of feet to the valley floor below.

There are several groups of peaks fulfilling *some* but not *all* of Valverde's conditions; and they can be looked upon, therefore, as false peaks which have lured many searchers astray. One magnificent group of "Three Peaks in the form of a triangle" we did come upon; and on its declivities, true enough, was a lake, a narrow outlet, and cascade. But other stipulations of Valverde's did not coincide.

One morning, however, our hopes ran high. While following a *cuchillo,* one of those long, narrow, knife-edged ridges, we came upon an extensive, clearly-cut depression. Broad, deep, and plainly marked, it followed a relatively straight course and gave every appearance of being the remains of an ancient roadway.

Enormously encouraged, we traced this out in both

directions, but at both ends it appeared to peter out, and the lay of the land offered no hope for a continuance nor reason for its existence. It may have been a natural freak geological formation or, if once a road, the surrounding country must have undergone some great cataclysm, and attempts on our part to follow the depression came to naught.

Shortly after this we came upon what is, I think without question, the source of the River Topo, which dashes in a violent winding course through the mountains to join the River Pastaza well to the south.

Our eyes were ever on the alert for geological specimens that might show signs of gold or other precious metal, but none did we see. In fact the whole region gave little evidence of being a gold-bearing country. Even if the ancients had thrown their treasure in a lake in the Llanganatis, they were en route from the mines at the time; and now more than ever I was convinced that if they existed, they must lie farther over on the eastern slopes.

The "Mountain of Margasitas" proved another delusion. No sign of any pyrites whatsoever did we find, until much later on, when I had passed beyond the eastern rim of the mountains.

Our daylight hours were filled with mapping, sketching, and forever seeking our main objective— a feasible pass through the mountains to the east to the head of the Curaray River and the Oriente.

By now we had mapped an enormous area and learned a great deal of the region. One thing now was certain. No feasible passageway to the Oriente lay on this line. A route further north must be sought.

In the course of this search we ranged through a vast new territory. For forty days we searched in vain. But at last good fortune favored us. For the first time we awoke to a beautiful clear day. After marching for about three hours Bill and I reached the top of a pass from which we could see the whole surrounding country. Before our incredulous eyes opened out a great indentation which seemed to cut through the barrier made by the mountain ranges, presumably to a river valley below. This gave every indication of a natural passageway to the east. If this proved to be so, our problem was solved.

We were congratulating ourselves, eagerly intent upon this discovery, when abruptly we saw something that had hitherto escaped us. To the left of where we were standing suddenly loomed a new "Three Peaks" —and right on the line given by Valverde! This confirmed in my mind my original belief that previous searchers had misread Valverde's directions, and had gone too far to the south.

One can imagine the surprise and encouragement which followed the glimpse of this pass through the mountains, heightened as it was by the sight of the new "Three Peaks." With all haste we prepared to get under way.

True, these peaks lay quite far north, in fact on the border of what is deemed by some to be the Llanganatis proper. The supposed confines of this region are most variable, and the origin of the name by no means certain. So far as I can tell, the first known use of the word "Llanganatis" is in the Valverde Guide, where he applies it to his particular Three Peaks of the treasure. There is an old Quechua word, Llanga, "to touch." It is quite plausible, therefore, that Valverde used it merely to indicate his *Three Peaks*, which were (llanganati) "touching" or "joined" together by their geological formation, and not as a name for the entire region.

As we were leaving to follow our new clew, the rain broke afresh, but the pendulum of luck was evidently swinging in our favor; for, scarcely had we started, when we managed to shoot four ducks. The dinner that followed was the best we had known in months in this region where game was so scarce.

The next day we went up a great valley, only to meet with a downpour that exceeded any we had so far encountered. The Fourth of July, that blistering hot holiday Bill and John had so familiarly known in the States, found us trapped in a pass on top of a *cuchillo*, with intermittent rain, snow, or sleet as our constant companions.

It was then that I felt obliged to give the "pep" talk of my life, and the outcome was that, after a lengthy palaver among themselves, the Indians decided to stick "just a little longer."

All around us was a dense thicket of chaparral which, though not high, was almost impenetrable. For example, Bill and I had to go down a hill face from our camp in the saddle of a mountain to the valley below. It was only a matter of a few hundred yards, yet it took over an hour and a half to cover.

Our objective was to find a way through to these new "Three Peaks," of which we now seemed to be within striking distance. After two days of effort, our reward was an impasse—a sheer drop impossible to descend or cross. I then turned my attention to trying to find a course over a saddle in the ridge to the southeast, but for several days I failed utterly.

The rain continued for three days more, and we were held as in a vise. Through most of this period we were unable to see twenty yards away, everything was afloat, and the valley floor had become a lake. But finally the weather relented, and on we shoved in bitter cold and sleet, eventually succeeding in reaching the saddle, which was our destination.

The weather continued to improve to such an extent that the next day we were able to reach the crest of the main peak, where the altimeter read 12,360 feet. I climbed to the far edge and looked expectantly down below. I was not disappointed. There, cradled in a declivity of the great peak, was a sheet of emerald-green glass—a lake—just as Valverde had described it!

Hastening back, I waved the men to a lower route. Eagerly we made camp on the saddle of the mountain and set out at once to explore the region. From a distance the surrounding country had appeared to be pleasant, easy grassland, but when we reached it we found it to be chaparral so high, tough, and dense that

Above: "Following now on foot in the same direction, . . ."
Typical Knife-Edge *Cuchillo*

Below: ". . . thou shalt see a mountain which is all of
margasitas, . . ." (Valverde Guide)

Above: "...and from thence thou shalt perceive the three Cerros Llanganati, in the form of a triangle..." (Valverde Guide)

Below: "...thou wilt come on a cañon between two hills, which is the Way of the Inca..." (Valverde Guide)

it required an hour to progress but a few hundred feet, its elasticity resisting every blow of our machetes.

Every yard was a struggle, but despite this we were greatly encouraged. Upon reaching the lip of the lake we found an outlet so narrow we could jump across it and below appeared a flashing cascade, "green pasture in a small plain" and a "cañon betwixt two hills" —all agreeing perfectly with the Guide.

In all our wanderings in the Llanganatis this setting was the only one we encountered that fulfilled so many of Valverde's stipulations. As a climax to it, high up on the mountain-side and dimly discernible to the eye, was a long, narrow depression for all the world like an ancient roadway.

Our hopes ran high, and excitement coursed through our veins, blinding us to the brutal truth. For, when I summed up the situation, I knew without doubt that the crisis had come. The transport animals had long since been sent back. Right after that all our Indians had abandoned the Expedition, as well as many of the peons. Such had been the ravages of the climate that of the original seventeen soldiers only seven remained in good enough physical condition for me to feel justified in asking them to continue further.

I had to face the truth. No more work could be expected of these men upon the lake regardless of what treasure might be hidden in its deep recesses. It meant infinite toil with fresh men, more supplies, and much apparatus. To do more than we had done was impossible.

The bitterness of the blow was great, but it had to be banished from our minds, as all thought had now to be given to the all-important problem of finding the pass through to the east.

It was a race against time. Food was appallingly low, and the percentage of men that were now too incapacitated to proceed farther was so high that I realized with foreboding I had but a day or two left in which to find this pass or be forced to give up the whole project after nearly a year in the field.

Time after time we scaled the surrounding peaks to try and catch those few moments of clarity which, in this atmosphere, when they do occur, come just after dawn.

It was a world of infinite solitude, doubly awe-inspiring from the fact that, lost in the constant mist but a few feet away, the mountains dropped into an abyss from the terrifying pinnacle on which we stood. Nothing but mist enveloped us. Bank after bank of heavy, rolling clouds clung to us as if determined to obstruct all our attempts. We could see nothing. We could learn nothing.

The time for a decisive step rapidly approached. I could not expect to hold the men longer.

That night I lay awake in my sleeping bag wondering what the morning would bring. We had traveled miles and miles in face of constant setbacks, and such a short distance remained to complete the last link in the chain to the frontier. Was ours just to be one more name to add to that lengthy list of failures?

After so long, defeat seemed impossible to accept.

Above: "... on whose declivity there is a lake made by hand, into which the ancients threw the gold ..."
Note One of the Three Peaks in Background

Below: The Resting Place of the Inca's Ransom?
E. Erskine Loch in Foreground in Typical Sheepskin Clothing Worn by the Expedition

The Long-Sought Pass; Gateway to the Oriente

Chapter XVI
DEATH AND NEAR DEATH

MORNING came to find us once again clambering up the steep ascent to the peak.

It seemed at last that a Hand mightier than our own was to reward our puny efforts. The fog lifted abruptly, and in the first clear moment in twenty-one days of almost continuous downpour we found ourselves staring at a panorama which thrills me even now in retrospect.

The atmosphere cleared for miles and miles around. It was a never-to-be-forgotten sight. Viewed through the crystal light from my pinnacle thousands of feet in the air, the great towers of Cotopaxi, Quilindaña, Torres, Yana Urcu, and Cerro Hermoso stood like a distant chain of fortresses guarding the whole country of the old Valverde Guide. Far off to the east stood the beautiful symmetrical cone of Sumaco. While peering across range after range of lower ridges, the eastern foothills of the Andes, I saw my destination, the Oriente. It extended for miles like a gargantuan bas-relief map; and there in the far distance lay my goal—the familiar Napo Valley, cliffs of the Arajuno, and the Curaray River. The sight set my blood tingling.

Photographs and compass bearings were taken with more eagerness than ever before. There was not a moment to lose, for the great banks of clouds soon rolled in to obscure our view once more. But I was elated. For during those few hectic moments I was convinced that I had seen, a little off to one side, the long-sought pass.

In a straight line the distance to the Napo Valley appeared to be sixteen to twenty miles at the most, and my enthusiasm was such that I felt nothing could hold me back. Little did I know that covering those sixteen or twenty miles was to occupy more than seventy days of hell which made all the previous misery seem as nothing.

From August 7th to 16th we laboriously cut our way down the side of the "Three Peak" group. Rain fell constantly; and, when we reached the river in the valley below and camped beside it, we found what had an hour before been a quiet mountain stream was now a raging torrent. Again we were faced with the familiar necessity of standing by with everything packed and ready for immediate evacuation. Hemmed in as we were with no means of escape because of the enclosing mountain-sides, we could not be too careful.

When we got under way next morning, we found the going more and more difficult; and the following day the river which we had been following entered a gorge, the sides of which were precipitous enough to bar the entry of even a wild mountain animal. Here was an impasse. It was so narrow and so deep that the foliage seemed to meet over the middle, giving the impression of a bottomless tunnel into which the river vanished from view in a boiling cauldron.

The only place we could find to camp was a minute *playa* in a small backwash where the stream over the centuries had eroded a flattened beach out of the sheer rock wall.

Bunched together in the congested space, our equipment rotting and the food mildewing despite our constant care, we faced a dismal night. Our anniversary since leaving New York—and what a place in which to celebrate it.

We named it Scorpion Camp, for here it was that George was badly stung by a scorpion. This was the price of reaching the more sheltered valleys beneath the crest of the peaks.

I knew now that our problem was so acute that there was but one solution, one that I had thrust from my mind as long as possible. But it had to be faced. Because of the shortage of carriers and of food it would be impossible to take the whole Expedition through. If the Oriente was to be reached, I would have to continue light.

I called for volunteer carriers among our few remaining soldiers and peons to take a chance with me on what lay ahead. Private Pons agreed instantly; and, through his example, two others quickly joined, a brother soldier, Pasmino, and Cajas, a peon.

Before me now lay the most unpleasant duty I had yet had to perform. How could I tell the loyal Expedition members who had come so far with me that they were to go no farther? After a year of the closest companionship and infinite work together toward our common ends, they were now to be robbed of the fruit of that labor through the exigencies of circumstance. I knew without asking that each was ready to follow, for there had never been a moment that their untiring efforts had shown any sign of weakening. To make this decision was the most painful duty I had ever had to perform.

The moment came, but it was easier than I had anticipated—they knew.

Leaving that cul-de-sac, we parted on the higher ground, they to retrace their steps to distant Pillaro and await me, the three carriers and I to climb the ridge, our eyes on the far Oriente.

My party was a polyglot lot, phantoms almost, strange and doubtless weird even to the birds. For weeks we had not shaved. Our sheepskins, tied in at the belt with ropes, made of us shapeless, bearlike figures moving through a Doré etching. Our trousers were hide chaps over whipcord riding breeches, both tucked into high field boots now scuffed and worn almost beyond recognition. A heavy cloth balmoral topped off my ensemble, and over this when the occasion demanded went a rough wool scarf wound round and round until at times my face was completely hidden save for my eyes.

The men were only slightly less grotesque. Squat, thickset Cajas was, but for his swarthy complexion and hawk-like appearance, a duplicate of myself. Pons and Pasmino, the Ecuadorean soldiers, were of more slender build; and I sometimes wondered how their thin frames managed to support the voluminous outer garments in which they were enveloped.

The country ahead was the most dangerous we had yet encountered. Spur after spur of precipitous rock faces descending almost perpendicularly into raging torrents below barricaded our passage. These bald surfaces, to which we were forced to cling, were covered by but a few inches of soil, out of which from the constant rains a heavy foliage grew, though with deceptively shallow roots. Everything we stood upon, everything we clutched, with the added weight of our loads, gave way under us to fall hundreds of feet to the plunging river below.

Yet in some way we managed to progress.

Each morning we would start out wondering what new disaster was awaiting. On one occasion there was a cry behind me, and on glancing around I saw Pons hanging over a precipice, dangling by his left arm from a small tree. Even as I looked, the tree began giving way under him. But fortunately his load snagged in some foliage, thus arresting his fall to what would have been certain death.

Another time Pasmino disappeared as though swallowed up. We worked our way carefully to the edge of the rock on which he had been standing and saw him in momentary safety on a ledge a few yards below. It was a good hour before we had pulled him to safety.

Still again Pasmino uttered a cry and, together with a mass of stunted shrubbery, slid slowly from sight. Everything at which he grasped gave way. There was a drop of some two hundred feet to the river from where he had been; and, when our calls to him were unanswered, I felt he was gone beyond saving.

But on clambering down we found him entangled in a broken tree, his load still intact. Yet the force of his fall had strained the tree to such an extent that he did not dare to move. Placing a rope around him, his load, and the tree all in the same bight, we finally hoisted them all to safety.

I was the next. While crossing a narrow ledge along a precipitous drop, the bulky haversack between my shoulders made me face the rock to work my way over. It was some twenty feet to the other side, and with considerable difficulty I had reached the middle. Suddenly I noticed that the small crevice in the rock face to which I was clutching so desperately, appeared to be moving slowly upwards. For the moment I could not understand the phenomenon, until I realized with a shock that it was not the rock that was moving, but the narrow ledge on which I stood. *That was sinking.*

I was many yards from safety at either end. And

powerless as I was to move, there was nothing I could do but watch as it slowly crumbled.

In less time than it takes to tell, I was in the air going headlong down the precipice.

For the moment that I was conscious I recall experiencing the first feeling of genuine relaxation I had known for months. It was a pleasant world of dreams in which nothing mattered. It was sublime.

The next thing I remember was being flat on my back with Cajas, who must of necessity have taken considerable time to work his way down to the bottom of the precipice, looking into my face and asking if I was hurt. At that moment I didn't think that I was, and the whole episode of being in the air had been really quite enjoyable—until I moved.

Then I felt a stabbing pain in the region of my lungs and another, more dull, in my right leg.

We had found from previous experience that a load will invariably turn a falling man in the air, at the same time acting as a cushion when he strikes. This had happened to me, for almost everything in my haversack was smashed. Yet unfortunately, in coming to a stop, a jagged point of rock had cut through the stout sack and had struck my spine, and two of my ribs were broken. My right leg also was badly injured. With the excessively deep breathing that is necessary at such altitudes, the injury to my lungs was the cause of incessant pain, which never left me for months to come. But the shortage of men made it necessary for me to continue carrying the weighty haversack as before. This, plus my leg injured in the fall, forced me to proceed with the aid of a stick. When confronted by rock faces I had to be pulled up by a rope. Thus the inexplicable curse of the Llanganatis, which had brought untold disaster to other expeditions, brought us to the very brink of catastrophe. Extraordinary ill fortune seemed to follow us; yet it was this which was in the end to bring me a piece of good luck so incredible I can scarcely believe it even now.

Our descent to the bottom of the valley took a week, and, on reaching the river bank, we found ourselves in a trap at the junction of two rivers.

One was fairly tranquil at this point for a mountain river, but broad—far too broad for us to bridge—while the other, narrow enough to permit bridging, was extremely turbulent and in flood. It was exceedingly swift and filled with huge water-worn rocks as slippery as ice. Although my heart sank as I considered the prospect, it appeared the easier of the two, and we fell to work on trying to span it. We commenced our bridge, but before we could make it fast it was lost in the foam. And so with another and another and another.

According to my diary we made seventeen attempts in all, each crude structure being swept away like its predecessors. Precious days were wasted, and eventually we were forced to turn to the broad river which, though too deep to ford, was calm at one place and gave us a chance to cross by raft with a rope.

We soon had knocked together a flimsy raft of

sorts and were ready to make the attempt. I feared that our cable was all too short for the broad span, but with the assistance of Cajas and Pons it was eventually stretched to the other bank and secured. This was made possible through Cajas' finding a foothold on a small rock in the middle of the swiftly moving river, while Pons poled and paddled himself across, held from being swept into the rapids by the cable, and was the first to set foot on the far bank. The cable had reached all right, but with little to spare.

Meanwhile, I had been lying on our side of the river directing them. Inability to shout instructions, owing to my injured lungs, necessitated my speaking them to Pasmino, who, in turn, would yell them across to Cajas. Then they were relayed to Pons, who signaled his arrival by a wave, for a short distance below this calm stretch was a cascade, the roar from which was deafening.

Once the ferry line was secure, Pons started back in the raft by means of a short safety rope looped around the cable and secured to the raft.

On our side we waited eagerly as he started, drawing himself along by his hands. He was perhaps halfway to the rock on which Cajas was waiting for him when suddenly the raft broke free. The safety loop either broke or came untied. Slowly the raft gathered momentum downstream carrying the helpless Pons toward the boiling rapids. The stream was too broad and the current even here was too strong to paddle the raft to shore before it would be swept into the maelstrom. Like most of the mountain people he could not swim. He called out desperately and our anxiety in that moment was intensified by knowing there was nothing we could do. We watched for what seemed an eternity, as he finally disappeared forever amid the rapids—a frail, bent figure, hands clutching the fatal raft.

We never saw him again, although Pasmino and I searched a long distance below the falls on both banks. Some time later we found the raft smashed almost beyond recognition.

I never discovered what made that safety loop break free, unless it was that it had been insecurely tied, because I had tested the rope well before he started across.

But now a second danger drew us urgently back up river, for the position of Cajas on the solitary rock was extremely precarious. A slight rise in the river would sweep him off after Pons.

Our cable, still lashed to the other bank of the river, was impossible to recover, and our raft gone. Only a few feet of rope were available from our loads, not nearly sufficient to throw out to Cajas.

Neither could we find vines long enough to make a rope with which his rescue could be effected. The best we could do was to tie a series of branches together, lashed by flimsy bark and the few pieces of rope we had, until we had achieved a crude "pole." Our plan was to point this cumbersome apparatus upstream and allow the descending current to carry it into place.

But for two hours our efforts were in vain.

The slimy face of the rock prevented Cajas from reaching out to grasp it as it drifted past. At the same time the rock was too slippery to permit the pole to lodge securely against it.

In the end there was no recourse except for Cajas to jump into the water and catch the end of the pole as it drifted by. Like Pons, he could not swim, nor would it have availed him much in the strong current, and I knew that it required great courage on his part to decide to make the attempt. However, decide he did; and with Pasmino and myself holding fast to our end of the pole, he leaped out and caught the other.

Almost immediately he disappeared in the swirling torrent, but we could tell that he was holding on with every ounce of strength he possessed. He seemed to weigh tons.

After a terrific struggle we eventually managed to swing him in to the bank where he clambered to safety.

Then followed as astonishing an example of the typical characteristics of the peon's mind as I have ever seen—a forgetfulness of danger that is almost animal-like the moment that danger is past.

Immediately after he was landed, the whole episode was gone from his mind—while for some time afterwards I broke into a cold sweat every time I thought about the close shave he'd had.

The night we spent in that camp there on the river was one of the most miserable of the entire expedition. The terrible physical and spiritual strain of the day made it impossible for me to lie prone on the hard, rocky ground, and I suffered the tortures of hell in trying to sleep in a sitting position. During the long hours before daybreak I could hear Cajas and Pasmino wailing in the darkness for the spirit of their lost companion.

During my sleeplessness I turned over in my mind the career of Private Pons since we had first come together. At first no one would have suspected that Pons was the strong character that he later proved to be. Of the seventeen volunteer soldiers supplied me by the government, he was the most useless, being quite unable to carry even a light load without becoming fatigued. In the mountains he was completely at a loss and could not retrace his own steps for even a short distance. If the other members of the Expedition got far in advance, he would be unable to follow them in the mist; and someone would have to be sent back to retrieve him. From the outset the others made him the butt of their jokes and later came to dislike him because of the extra work he caused. He was ridiculous, almost grotesque—the "ugly duckling."

But I kept him on despite his shortcomings, for his life was wrapped up in the project. Totally unfitted by nature and physique for such arduous work as we had to do, yet by some strange, inexplicable twist in his mentality, he thought of nothing save the opportunity given him to follow wherever I might lead. It seemed to me that his sole ambition in life was to see the Andes-Amazon Expedition through to a successful conclusion.

As time went on, he created such a prejudice among the others that I took pity on him and made him my personal assistant in charge of the camp and equipment, a position for which he proved himself to be most admirably suited. Working directly under me, he was in his element. Previously he had been browbeaten, ridiculed, and despised; and even in his regiment he had again and again risen by slow degrees, only to be demoted back to the ranks for some blunder.

But now he was a "somebody" and in his own estimation the most important member of the party next to myself. He became a self-respecting man, held his head up, and endeavored in every way to repay the trust I placed in him after I had promoted him. Never did he complain of those long, weary marches, of the rain or cold, snow or bitter wind.

This rise in status for Private Pons had a curious effect. Where before he had been cautious almost to the point of inadequacy, now he was the one to inspire the others by his willingness to face danger.

On the day when I had called for volunteers, Pons was the first to step forward. By his action he also inspired Pasmino and Cajas to join me. For the rest of the terrible journey that lay ahead these three men had been my only companions, and to them I owe whatever success we achieved.

This is true most of all in the case of Private Pons, for I must freely confess that a short time before his death, considering my now reduced powers owing to my accident and the constant failure of the bridges, I gave way to doubt. I began seriously to consider giving up. I knew that once across this stream, which had now become our Rubicon, to return would be well-nigh impossible.

This was the only occasion during the whole course of the Expedition when I ever entertained the thought of turning back. To do so seemed so easy—I found myself making every excuse for it. Just then Pons entered my shelter. He was radiant with optimism. He talked lengthily of the spring that he felt sure was about to break and the better weather to which we could look forward. There was something in his enthusiasm as he continued that made me ashamed. I was afraid to tell him what was in my mind, and I made a quick decision to go forward, from which I never swerved again.

So, without his ever being aware of the part he played, it was really Private Pons who swayed the Expedition's course.

At the crossing of the river, when I could not move, he had become the self-appointed leader—the inspiration for the others. His undying tenacity of purpose and his enthusiasm were contagious as he rose to new heights of self-reliance. He had become far more than my assistant—he had become my friend. From the ugly duckling, despised and ridiculed, Pons grew to merit and receive our respect, admiration, and love. His death was a terrible blow, one which cast a pall over all the rest of the Expedition.

Yet looking back and knowing as I do that after leaving me he would have had to return to the army a mere soldier, inconspicuous and obscure, it is some consolation to know that Pons died at the very apex of his life.

Chapter XVII
FAMINE

THE best record of the days that were to follow is contained in my diary, which I wrote on the spot and from which the following excerpts are taken:

September 4—Union Camp. Alt.: 5860'.

Beautiful morning, thank the Lord. Really looks as if spring has come at last. The luck of having a sunny morning with the extraordinary effect it has on us all, and we make a last attempt to cross the smaller river. If we fail now we can't possibly go on as we must keep the remaining food to try and get back to safety the way we came. We reach the river and to our delight for the first time it has dropped low enough to try another bridge. A boulder has shown up in the middle which, although only a few inches above the foam, will demand a much shorter span. Spend the whole day doing this and in the late afternoon finally succeed in getting a flimsy bridge across. The best we can do is one foot above the water level just above a terrific cascade. The stream is so powerful here that if it strikes your foot in passing while the bridge bends low under your weight you would be swept off in a moment. Damn. Too late now to cross tonight as it is nearly dark and will be too risky; we still have a difficult climb back to camp. Hope to God no rain comes tonight, for a slight rise will sweep our flimsy bridge away. This is our eighteenth attempt to bridge the river. Periodically throughout the day we cooeed for Pons. Not a sign of an answer. I'm afraid there isn't a chance for him now. We return to camp at dusk with a feeling of great encouragement though, having got a bridge across at last, and the hope that spring has come. It seems too bad that this had to happen just one day after Pons was lost. All feel full of hope for tomorrow.

September 5—Union Camp 2—M. R. Camp No. 1.
Alt.: 5790'.
Fine last night and this morning. Had noticed an early dew for the first time in this camp. All of us get up with unusual cheerfulness, hoping against hope to leave this hated spot forever. By common accord none of us mentions Pons, yet I know we're all thinking of him as in removing from our loads all unnecessary things, we leave behind some of Pons' also. We leave the tent fly and our sheepskins. I went on ahead to the bridge while the others followed with their loads. The men can still travel

faster than I. God knows what's ahead of us. This crossing is a definite step, for I know damn well that once on the other side at the pace we are going I'll never get back if we don't get through. Must confess in my heart that I am afraid as hell of the crossing and prefer to try it alone. The now constant pain throughout my whole body since my fall has made me afraid of heights. Leave the foul, ill-fated Union Camp with mixed feelings, and reach the river. The bridge is intact, but desperately close to the water and the flimsy poles much too slippery to stand on with heavy nailed boots, so have to negotiate it astride with my feet hanging down. At lowest point of span my weight with the haversack bends the bridge down until I can hardly keep my feet out of the water, which is still falling over the cascade with great force. Great effort to keep from being spun round the slippery pole by the water and thrown into the cascade. Crossed to the eastern bank of the river at last and await the others. Finally both Cajas and Pasmino and our loads are all on the eastern bank of the bloody river, which we have all come to loathe. I estimate that we have traveled about 1500 yards in a straight line in the last 14 days. Great joy among us when we finally conquered this river. How we hated the damn thing. It has really taken us since August 17th (20 days) to find our way through the short impasse. At 10 A.M. we leave and continue along the south bank of the bigger river which flows to the east. A great change here—mostly easy playa [beach]. One easy rise where we had to ascend and we reached the water's edge again. We keep calling for Pons all the way down from the union, but no answer. We explore ahead and it appears to be nothing but playa, but on the north bank of the river it is absolutely perpendicular and quite impassable. This we couldn't see from the union. What good fate that we didn't try that way. Men and myself in best of spirits now that we are across. Beautiful day and looks like a promising night. River bed at this point 60 to 70 yards across but current here about 12 miles an hour. Very rocky and shows signs of a 6-foot flood rise. Altitude this camp at 5:30 P.M. 5790'. Beautiful night. But in spite of better conditions suffered the worst pain I have yet had. Something must be wrong, for the pain has lasted so long.

Sunday, September 6th—M. R. Camp No. 1 to No. 2.

Leave camp and continue along rocky beach. Banks chiefly wooded playa and the boulder beach seems wonderfully easy going after what we've been used to. Although we had to cross half a dozen small "noses" there was nothing serious today. During the day we saw a cock of the rock—another good sign of the Oriente. Estimated distance traveled today 1800 yards, and a damned good coverage. Alt.: 5:30 P.M., 5560'.

September 7th—M. R. Camp No. 2 to No. 3.

Rained until dawn but cleared at daybreak. Stopped by rock ahead at the bend of the river. A road would have to be blasted around this. We climb up 100 feet or more and descend again to the beach by the early afternoon. Camped tonight in a pleasant open playa which appears to continue on both banks for some distance. H. E. distance traveled today about 650 yards. Alt.: 5350′.

September 8th—M. R. Camp No. 3 to No. 4.

Very bad pain in back and chest during night. Seems to be getting worse. Soon after leaving camp this morning continue along the playa by the river. See a snake track in the sand—the first I've seen in these parts. Later on in the morning we see many large tapir tracks—some quite fresh. Today the best yet and by far the easiest going—very encouraging for the future. All over open rock playa. Probably did 3 kms. [1½ miles]. By the afternoon decide to camp. While men are preparing camp, I push on a little bit further. To my surprise I find another river flowing in from our side within 50 yards of camp although it is invisible from it. There is no doubt about it—very black water which colors the previously bright green of the waters of our river from here on. Low at present and easily bridged. Go back to camp and break the news to the men that they've *got* to cross tonight. Cannot risk another flood. Make a temporary bridge and by 6 P.M.

are across on the east side of the river with all
loads. Caught by the dark and have to sleep in a
hurried, foul camp as consequence—very different
from the comfortable one we were in the other side
of the river. Much blaspheming from the men, but
thank the Lord we crossed tonight, for at 9 P.M.
heavy rain starts and continues until dawn.

September 9th—M. C. No. 4 to No. 5.

Overcast at dawn but rain has ceased. Altitude,
5:30 A.M., 4780′. Thank God below 5000 feet for
the first time. Thank God also I insisted on men
crossing last night. It is down in tremendous flood
this morning and our bridge swept away. What a
break! If we hadn't crossed it looks as if we'd been
held up another 3 days on the other side. Great les-
son to the men always to cross a river while you
can. I rubbed it well in to stop their grousing. At
6:30 A.M. I start off ahead of the others as I can
still only travel very slowly. Others follow about 7.
About 8:30 A.M. we strike a high impassable perpendicular cliff that drops vertically down into the
river. Cannot see how far it extends. No way round
down below. Start to cut a trail over the top. Rain
comes on. First attempt fruitless although we climb
very high. The rock is still perpendicular near the
edge. It appears to be on the end of a very big spur.
It is too late now to hope to pass it today, so we
returned back to a point near our previous camp
where we spent the night. River suddenly comes

down in big flood. This side of the water very black so the tributary we crossed must be getting a second flood. This is another beastly camp—wet and congested, though at least fairly level. Alt.: 4610′.

September 10th—M. C. No. 5 to No. 6.

We rise well over 200 feet in a general southerly direction to avoid the precipice. Nasty dangerous climb but finally descend to the beach on the other side from which I can see that we have traveled, according to land marks on opposite bank, exactly 100 yards beyond the point we reached yesterday. But now we are on the east side of the rock. Not much distance covered today. Rained tonight. Alt.: 4510′.

September 11th—M. C. No. 6 to No. 7.

Raining at dawn but stopped soon afterwards, and remained overcast during the day. We continue along river but by 10:30 A.M. we are stopped by another rock bank. Make several attempts here. Fail to get past today. We go into camp. Started raining in the afternoon. Everything so wet we make no dinner. Alt.: 4390′.

September 12th—M. C. No. 7 to No. 8.

Overcast and very damp at dawn. Men terribly pooped this morning—very hard to get them up. Have to cut down the loads today to save them. Almost immediately after leaving camp this morning we strike the cliff and try a higher course. Have to rise 100 feet or more but find we cannot get down on the other side. Constant necessity of dumping loads to cut our way through and going back for the loads doubles the distance. Cliff and landslides the worst yet. Finally get down about 2:30 P.M. Going much easier. Camp at No. 8 about 5:30 P.M. Hills much more open and spread apart here. It really looks like the approach of the flat country of the Oriente and, I hope, the junction of the Jatun Yacu (upper Napo), which we are seeking. Fine all day today but for a few thunder storms in the afternoon. There have been several lately. Alt.: 4220'.

September 13th—M. C. No. 8 to No. 9.

Fine night but started to rain at dawn. Continue along playa until the end of the observation shot I had taken where we meet a rock again. Mapping here awfully difficult through lack of getting clear shots, and having to leave river so constantly because of these obstructing spurs. This rock not so bad and we soon reach the playa again. Soon after midday strike an impassable place at what turns out to be a canyon through which the River flows. Absolutely sheer on both banks. Have to dump all loads and cut our way over the top, but finally reach the river bank again on the other side by 3:30 P.M. after the stiffest and most dangerous climb yet over these "noses." Men awfully done up today, and the hills surrounding the gorge seem very high and steeper than ever. Damn disappointing after the open appearance of the country yesterday. Pasmino crossed himself with thankfulness on reaching the beach again after scaling this rock, which was our worst yet. Rained during the night. Alt.: 4050'.

September 14th—M. C. No. 9 to No. 10.

Everyone terribly done-up today and after the very dangerous crossing of the nose yesterday I had promised the men a late sleep this morning so didn't get off until 10 A.M. Country is desperate now—the men awfully tired. Country eases out a little and we strike mostly playa again until going around the bend where we are completely held up. Out of the question to pass by the river. Dumped loads and spent 2 hours cutting this afternoon, but still quite impossible to get over on the line we have picked—too steep. At 5 P.M. we have to come down and return, having failed to get through. Are forced to make camp in a few square feet in an old tree root. Beds have to be pegged in; suspended 40 or 50 feet above the river. Damn dangerous; everywhere precipitous. Our worst camp yet. But today the Corporal had the closest shave of being killed that he's had yet. Returning down the precipice he fell and couldn't check his fall. Went at a tremendous speed toward the river 100 feet below. Everything he grabbed broke under him. Finally by the grace of God he struck a tree that held him just long enough for us to get him up again. Very badly scared and shaken. What a bloody country. Two bits of good news though. The altimeter at 7 P.M. 40 feet above the river stands at 3860—below 4000 at last. Also Cajas shot a "gallina de las cierras," but we are all too tired to cook it tonight. No thunder storms tonight but the "voices of the river" are constant; dogs barking, too, on the other bank. Extraordinary how these imaginary voices call, and call, and call one all the time. The same with the dogs barking. Drives you mad. I know it's imagination, but ever since Pons' death and the gloom cast over the camp by my accident, I know that even the men hear them too. Several times I have seen Cajas stop and listen as if to someone calling him. Must be sounds caused by the water. Constant night after night of pain, and sleeping always beside the foul rushing waters of the river on ground that is constantly vibrating from the rush of the water as one lies in bed, affects one. Rushing water without ceasing, and far-away voices always calling—I wonder whether we are all going off our heads. One feels it all the worse after "bad moments" over these dangerous rock faces. We are really scared to death half a dozen times a day—all of us. Had one or two dreams that I am no longer in the Llanganatis Mountains and wake up to find that I am still here. I suppose when I do get out I will have nightmares that I am back again! [Note: Curiously enough, for the first three nights after I had reached safety, I actually did have these nightmares of being back in these moun-

tains. Pasmino told me he had the same.—E. E. L.]
We must get through soon or God knows. Desperately little food left at all now, and all of us dreadfully done-up. The Curaray River all seems a century ago—almost as if it never had happened. Camp No. 10 and still no sign of the Napo.

September 15th—M. C. No. 10 to No. 11.

Hell of a night and hell of a camp, but we cooked the "gallina de la cierros" that Cajas shot yesterday and God what a difference it makes to all of us. It reminds one of food again. Day becomes overcast. A late start this morning owing to the gallina but we get off by 9, and reach the beach on the other side of the "nariz" by 11. All of us so done-in today that by 2:30 we have to stop. Mapping has been desperately difficult the last few days. River has narrowed now but full of very large boulders which, on the beaches at the side, have also increased in size. Every few yards one has to get down one several feet in height and each time my bloody pack bumps against my injured back. We are all desperately sick of this now. Alt.: 3770'.

September 16th—M. C. No. 11 to No. 12.

No rain last night and looks like a beautiful day. We all leave at 6:30 A.M. Many little "narizes" to cross but nothing bad so far. Rain came on at noon very heavily and held us up. Bank of river very steep here. Precipitous on both banks. Finally after rising and descending we get caught in a cul-de-sac at 5 P.M. and have to spend another foul night in a "tree trunk" camp. Alt.: 3590'.

September 17th—M. C. No. 12 to No. 13.

Overcast on awakening. Leave camp at dawn and strike for the top of the ridge to get out of the cul-de-sac, hoping desperately to find some signs of Indian trails. With the exhausted state that everyone's in and the number of landslides and fallen trees, we hardly make any time at all; 100 yards an hour is our very best. While going up the ridge at one moment I thought Pasmino was finished. He looked ghastly and with what energy he did have left he was on the verge of mutiny. Frightened, too, that this was the end. If he had had a gun —I know what he felt like doing to me. Strange when people are frightened how they turn against the person who started it all. By 1 P.M. we have risen up to 4520, nearly 1000 feet above our last camp. From this point I can see that the spur that we are on runs a great distance to the north where there is a big depression of what I hope to God is the union of our river with the upper Napo (Jatun Yacu). It looks like a big detour in the river. We can never make it in our state. Must take a chance and go over the top to the east, hoping that the river on the other side is the Jatun Yacu. No food now since we had the gallina because the bloody fool Cajas somehow threw away the dehydrated vegetables and brought along some coffee in exchange. Nothing left at all. At the last crevasse Cajas fell and injured his leg. Hope to God he is all right tomorrow, but he doesn't seem to be able to move it now, so we go into camp. Reckon that we are about 2000 yards due south of the beginning of the great depression which I hope is the union of the rivers. According to all calculations it should be. If we don't strike the Jatun Yacu tomorrow we are off the line somewhere and it's a bad fix. Camp at No. 13 at 5 P.M. Today I had to be pulled up two cliff faces with a rope, Cajas, as usual, doing damn good work balancing on a flimsy tree trunk. Fine night. Alt.: 4680'.

September 18th—M. C. No. 13 to J. Y. No. 1.

No rain last night and looks like a fine morning. First bit of news of the day is that Cajas says his leg is paralyzed and that he cannot move it at all. Nonsense. Hell of a place to get incapacitated in. We've got to get through to the Napo. He just feels like saying it. Good old Cajas and, sure enough, by 7 A.M. we are off, and he seems to have forgotten all about it. But lord, what a change from our hopes. Everybody falling for absolutely no reason. I'm sure we've still got a great struggle ahead to get to the Napo and, true enough, this was the worst day we've had. It seems a hopeless effort, yet we finally reach the top of the spur at over 5000 feet. Going down on the other side is easy in comparison until descending the valley we are stopped by a precipice which, on looking over, is part of a deep gorge. Upon approaching the edge we can see a river down below which ought to be the Napo, but my God it's only 30 yards wide. It seems impossible that this is the Napo into which all the upper water-shed has flowed. Awful doubts that we are wrong. In this country of enormous detours it is possible that it is another curve of *our* river and that we are still on the damn thing. If it is, the Napo must be on the far side of the big range we see to the north and we'll never make it now. I can't understand this, as all calculations seem correct. If we are cut off by this now we are done. The men are almost finished and all the food long since gone. Curse Cajas and his bloody coffee. 4 P.M. now, so camp at the edge of the precipice. Altitude here 3390. A foul camp, balanced in a tree root again. Not a single square inch level. Rain without ceasing the whole night. Impossible for any of us to sleep with everything soaking wet—just to make things easier. Desperate night of doubts. Can't understand where our calculations could be wrong. Daren't tell the others of my doubts.

September 19th—J. Y. No. 1 to No. 2.

Still raining at dawn. Everything soaking. Feel desperately ill this morning; don't know why. Decide to leave everything behind here and make a dive for it. In going through my stuff I find a bottle of George Brun's blasted cough mixture.

God knows how it got there. So short of food that I drink the remains of it for it seemed sweet with some glycerine stuff in its mixture. It made me sick a few minutes after. Try and keep the spirits of the men up by showing much more confidence than I really feel that this is the Napo River. It seems so unbelievably small. If it isn't we are certainly done for. We leave soon after dawn and follow the line of the river as best we can. Extremely hard to map the river from this height above it, which we cannot approach because of the deep gorge through which it is flowing. We make hopeless time. Never known anyone to travel as slowly as we are. We can hardly cross one leg in front of the other. When we fall our legs literally will not move to pick us up again although we honestly try to do so. On one occasion I must have been down for quite a few minutes before my legs would function at all. Everything rotten to the hold with the recent rains. About 10 A.M. we reach a ravine with a chorrera [rivulet stream] falling precipitously down into the river. A very dangerous descent. Last bit falls over a very bad landslide. Still wet and slippery from the rain. In crossing this bloody place the ledge gives way under me. Thank God for two hanging vines. Catch them just in time and hang there swinging. I can't hang on long in my damaged state, and good old Cajas risks his life, climbs down to the broken edge, breaks off an improvised hook from a branch which he hooks

around the vines. With this he swings me backwards and forwards until he finally swings me into
safety on that part of the ledge that wasn't broken
where he was standing. Bloody country this. Soon
after we crossed to the other side. During the afternoon both Cajas and the Corporal have tremendously close shaves again, falling and rolling over
the precipice to be caught just in time on a tree
root. We can hardly use our legs at all now. By
3 P.M. we reach a small 12-foot stream where we
are so done up that we have to stop and make the
only thing that we have left—about half a handful
of tea between the three of us. Still not a sign of
Indian life and another foodless night is before us.
This is a bad camping spot beside the stream so we
push on over the gentle rise on the other side to find
a better place. A short time later we see something
across the river that makes us all yell for joy—
an Indian—immovable and expressionless, just
watching us. He is the first human being we
have seen in all this time. We yell ourselves
hoarse to him across the gorge, "Jatun Yacu?
Jatun Yacu?" [Napo River? Napo River?] With
scarcely a movement he flicks his finger at his
feet where the river flows below us. It is the
Napo River after all, we are right on our line,
and in the Oriente at last! Never shall I forget
this feeling of relief. Although he cannot help
us at all with food from the other side of the river,
which has now broadened out, we push on, tre-

mendously encouraged, now hardly minding where we sleep that night. But as we descend a slope we see before us a sight of sights—signs of old cultivation grown over by the jungle—a disused Indian chacra [plantation]. We push through it excitedly and in the middle we find an abandoned Indian house. It has not been used for a year or two but old Cajas with rare instinct pokes into the rafters and finds, of all things, some dried maize which had been left behind by the former occupants. A little further afield we find the remains of a yuca patch still growing. What a windfall! None of us could wait until either the yuca or the maize was roasted at the fire which we soon got going. We started gnawing on the raw, dried maize without sitting, and later gorged ourselves on the roasted yuca. I think it was the best meal I have ever eaten—and a house to stay in for the night in good condition though not used for a year! Heavy rain came on at 4:30 but we didn't care a damn. We were in a house at last and with bursting stomachs. What a different feeling to an hour ago. Altitude 5 P.M. 3390' (a good height above the river).

Six days later we struggled, tattered, exhausted, but overjoyed, into a white settler's house—just seventy days after viewing that long-sought pass through the mountains from the top of our "Three Peaks." We were out!

Nearing the End
Cajas (*left*) and Pasmino (*right*) hear "The Voices"

Above: Crossing a Rocky *Playa*
Below: In the Oriente at Last
Abandoned Shelter, the First Sign of Indians

Chapter XVIII
AT THE RAINBOW'S END

THE house, a fine structure for those outlying parts, stood beside the river in a broad and fertile valley, the first fringe of civilization in the Oriente.

It was midday when we arrived; and, breaking in unheralded, we found Señor X——, the owner, at lunch in company with several other white men. With haggard face and heavy beard, no one at first knew who I was. But when they did and associated me with the newspaper stories that had originated in Quito so long before and heard the details of what we had been through, what a reception they gave me.

It was true that we had arrived foodless, yet with the forethought of my Scottish forebears, I had carried with me through the mountains a little wad of Ecuadorean money safely cached in my bandolier. Pulling out the now sodden mass, the bills virtually glued together, I offered those two splendid fellows, Pasmino and Cajas, anything they might choose to eat from the stock available.

"Puerco! A pig!" Nothing less would do, and instantly a fire was prepared. It would be a *muy grande* feast.

But an hour later we were rolling about in agony, from the unaccustomed plethora of good food. Especially Pasmino, who had eaten a strip of the hide raw —for "good luck."

Cajas, a typical mountain *cholo* (cross-breed) type, caused considerable interest among the Indians of the house, who were all of the Oriente.

What a strange sensation it was to sit there at a table surrounded by a ring of friendly, hospitable faces. Señor X— was particularly warm in his greeting.

As the meal went on, civilized life returned with each course, but as I looked about the group of four or five employees, a thought suddenly struck me— "Why should so many of them be here?"

My host was the only man living on this river and was a day's travel from the nearest little township. What brought so many of them to this outlying spot? And evidently just arrived?

I put the question.

"Ten of my Indians ran away and were reported in this neighborhood," said one.

I made no comment, for I had met him once before, and I was sure that with his slender resources he had never "owned" any Indians, let alone ten.

"Are you here on business?" I turned to a second.

He glanced across the table, reluctant to answer.

Then he coughed nervously. "Cattle," he said. "I am buying cattle."

I let that pass. He was a man from the mountains, which I knew to be a far better place in which to buy cattle than any such distant place as this.

The answers of the other three were equally vague. Yet all the time there had been no lack of friendliness in their manner. They seemed to be awaiting some signal from Señor X—, who continued to smile at me, but offered nothing to satisfy my curiosity.

I let the whole matter drop. After all, it wasn't my affair. The important thing was that those plunging cataracts and great canyons of the Llanganatis were behind me. And though an arduous trip back to Quito and the outside lay ahead, it seemed nothing to me now.

We lingered for two days' more rest, then set off, our friendly host accompanying us along the trail to see us well on our way. As we rounded a turn I waved good-by. He stood there watching me. A hand was running up the side of his face, and his features wore a look of indecision. I got the immediate impression that more was going on in his brain than he allowed to show on his brown, weatherbeaten face.

Civilization drew nearer with each step, and within a short time I was jogging along on a mule lost in thoughts of hot shower baths, fresh clothing, friends, theaters, dinners, New York.

It was with a feeling of great satisfaction that I glanced back along the trail at those mountains which for so long had impeded our progress. In spite of the difficulties of the pass, dynamite judiciously employed along the route would easily open a broad avenue and convert what had been for me days of travel into a feasible passage requiring but a few hours.* It was a year and four months since we had sailed from New York for Ecuador. All the original objectives of the Andes-Amazon Expedition had been accomplished.

We had explored and mapped a vast area of the Oriente, and had discovered that that great river, the Curaray, previously disregarded, forms a completely navigable waterway, and should become in the future a main artery of communication through Ecuador's Oriente to the outside world. By finding the long-sought pass through the Llanganatis, we had achieved the main objective for which the Expedition had gone out—to determine a more direct route than the present one from the civilized sections of Ecuador to the Amazon.

I looked forward eagerly to my reunion with John, George, and Bill. Each one had done his damndest— and well I knew it.

Our records show that out of the eight months spent in the mountains, only nine days had been clear. The Expedition in all traveled 2,280 miles on foot, horseback, in canoes, and on rafts. Our altitude had ranged between 795 feet and 14,800 feet above sea level, through areas totally devoid of food supplies.

* At first this may seem incredible, in view of the difficulties we had met. However, the brief analysis of the terrain in Appendix B will demonstrate this.

My thoughts turned in gratitude to the members of the Expedition, who had toiled amid tropical heat and rain, biting winds and snow; living it, working in it, sleeping in it. There's no romance to this, nor to a battle—while one takes part in it. Great physical effort and discomfort are one's sole companions.

Only with the passage of time, when one can relive past scenes amid a life of ease, does the spirit of romance transform those memories into something glamorous and picturesque.

And so the story of the Andes-Amazon Expedition was drawing to its close. Ahead lay Quito and beyond, New York.

A week later I was in my hotel in Quito. Around me lay bags, packing cases, clothes for the ocean voyage; and in my pocket were my passport and ticket. Northward bound from Peru, the Santa Lucia drew closer with each passing minute to Guayaquil to take me home.

For the first time in almost two years, I stretched back languidly in an armchair. My eyes closed. It was fine to be back in civilization.

Something roused me. I listened again. It was my telephone. I picked up the receiver. There was someone in the lobby to see me.

Who? A Señor X—? What could he be doing here so far from his home on the other side of the mountains? I was still half asleep when he stepped into my room.

What was he saying? I could scarcely believe my ears. Nor would he repeat what he had said.

Instead he opened a parcel he had carried under his arm and dumped out its contents. I gasped!

Gleaming dully before me lay the finest collection of gold nuggets I had ever seen in my life. Some of good size, others smaller, yet approximately more than three pounds—a modest fortune.

I was awake on the instant.

But where? How? What?

He smiled at my astonishment.

"It happened just before you appeared . . . in a bank across the river . . . the heavy rains . . . ! We found one, and another, then another! The rains that delayed you so long have been good to us." He leaned closer to me. "To both of us."

"Us?" I asked. "What do you mean?"

He smiled again. "I could not tell you at the time, because I had only found one nugget. While you were in my house I could not dig. But after you had gone, these others came to light. I followed at your heels to tell you, but I did not catch you until now."

I ran my fingers among the gleaming particles. Why, these were the finest ever discovered in Ecuador in modern times! Suddenly my heart missed a beat, for among them lay something of minute proportions. Then I found three more. Incredulously I picked them up for closer examination.

"Golden fishhooks," he said.

"Or parts of a broken ornament," I cut him off.

"Here's something more." He handed me a tiny hammered square of beaten gold.

Though infinitesimal in size, how much they meant! For they were conclusive proof that at some early time man had been there before.

Who could they have been? Pre-Incas, Incas, early Spaniards? I questioned him. He shrugged.

"My mother has known the district for many, many years and her mother before her. But they know nothing of any people who mined gold in that region. It must have been the ancients.

"But why do you bring these to me?"

His face lighted. "When you appeared that day from the Llanganatis, it seemed to me an omen that destiny had brought you my way just as I had found the first nugget. I trust you. I have no money to do this myself. I need help. Will you come and look?"

Weeks later, I returned to the spot, accompanied by a mining engineer, who will for obvious reasons remain anonymous, as must the well-known American mining company he represented. Prospecting pits were soon sunk in all directions around the "find"; picks and shovels rose and fell; shaft timbers went down into place; pumps clanked incessantly. No one let up for even a minute.

But our hopes were doomed. Barren, absolutely barren—the pits told their own story.

Yet this seemed impossible to accept. Such remarkable nuggets! Such a find! Those parts of an ornament, and hammered gold plate—they must mean something. But what?

I paused to realize that though much of the finest gold work is found in tombs or graves far from known deposits of the metal, yet these fragments were definitely closely associated with the nuggets. This proved the likelihood that since the nuggets and ornaments were found together man *must* have been there before. If there was a gold deposit of any great size somewhere in the neighborhood which had been worked by these early peoples, it was to be assumed that there would have been a settlement close at hand.

I looked around, pondering on what was hidden in the jungle growth around me. Was I standing on the very mine itself? Was it a stone's throw away?

At this juncture the mining engineer played his part.

Feverishly we widened the arc of our search. Upstream offered us nothing. Downstream was no better. But we were in no mood to desist.

Two weeks we spent at this work, and finally the mining engineer came into his own. He found signs of a densely packed gravel, an old gravel—far older than the others nearby. An ancient dried-up river bed unmistakably.

It carried gold!

Eagerly we followed it, cutting our way through the undergrowth only to lose it, and find it, then lose it, yet find it again more promising than before. It branched off into the jungle and tracing it care-

"Gold is where you find it"

The Rainbow's End

fully, by digging pits as we went, we followed it eventually to the junction of two small streams, where we came on an overgrown depression.

It seemed to mark a dike and canal system by which at some early time these streams had been diverted. That encouraged us to push ahead.

Looking up, we saw trees merging in the jungle that gave indication that the surroundings had once been under cultivation. Old stone implements, pieces of broken pottery, and a fragment of obsidian cutting stone came to light. Our belief now turned to certainty.

They were without doubt old gold workings.

Prospecting pits were sunk once again. Deeper and deeper they got and higher came the values. Finally we reached the bottom and found our reward—the gold, coarse and heavy, lay at bedrock.

Examination proved that the gold assayed at 21 carat, and the largest nuggets found ran up to 37 grams, a weight which carries a joyful indication that —*they have not traveled far from their source!*

Naturally, at this time I can not state what our prospecting will disclose, but I can say with absolute knowledge that this remarkable old river bed which is carrying the gold, contains somewhere in its length the motherlode. We had learned that the higher Llanganatis showed little indications of being a gold-bearing region. This confirmed my original belief that if the legend of Valverde be true, the ancient Incas were en route from some hidden gold mines to the *east* of the cordilleras when they heard of Atahualpa's death and cast their ransom into the "treasure lake." This region, then, is where the gold must lie.

Can it be that my most sanguine hopes are justified at last? Will it be that here on the fringe of those Llanganatis Mountains where I stood is one of the sources of those vast quantities of gold which brought ruin to the Inca Empire?

The Expedition's story seems to sweep backwards before me in panorama. The mists, clouds, floods, and famine of those great mysterious mountains now seem as nothing. The pestilential trip to Rayo Urcu, the Peruvian-Ecuadorean frontier, the heat, the flies, the fevers of the Curaray—all fade from my mind. I seem to stand again, dreaming, on the steps of the Public Library as in that spring of 1935. But now the dream is true.

The ancient dried-up river bed holds out promise of that golden reward which has lured me and countless others through four hundred years of search down the lost trail of the ancient "Derrotero," following the beckoning spirit of old Valverde towards his Llanganatis Treasure.

Appendix A
CONDENSED STATISTICS OF THE FIELD WORK OF THE EXPEDITION

TERRITORY EXPLORED
From the snow peaks around Ambato and Latacunga directly eastward across the Mulatos and Llanganatis Mountains and down the Curaray and Napo Rivers to the Peruvian frontier in the Oriente.

MAPPED
360 miles of rivers in the Oriente.
The Llanganatis and Mulatos Mountains.

TRAVELED
840 miles in canoes and rafts on rivers.
1440 miles on foot and horseback.

RECORDED
184 astronomical observations, 3200 survey angles and bearings, 714 altitudes, hygrometric, and thermometric readings.

RADIOED

21,000 odd words of communications from field camps to stations in Ecuador and the United States.

EXPOSED

605 still photographs.

COLLECTED

180 miscellaneous ethnological specimens, 470 ornithological and mammalogical specimens.

EMPLOYED

477 men and 58 animals during field period.

ALTITUDES AND TEMPERATURES WORKED IN

From 795 ft. to over 14,800 ft. (a.s.l.) and from minus 8 degrees centigrade at a humidity of 65% to a plus 35 degrees centigrade at a humidity of 85%.

COLLECTIONS AND REPORTS DISTRIBUTED TO

The Museum of the American Indian, New York City (Heye Foundation).

American Museum of Natural History, New York City.

Academy of Natural Sciences of Philadelphia.

Field Museum of Natural History, Chicago.

New York Zoological Society, New York City.

Central Park Zoo, City of New York.

American Geographical Society.

Royal Geographical Society, London, England.

Royal Scottish Geographical Society, Edinburgh, Scotland.

Appendix B

A FEW NOTES ON ECUADOR

ECUADOR IS SITUATED between Colombia and Peru on the northwest shoulder of South America directly on the equator, from which fact it derives its name. The country consists of two main divisions: Ecuador proper—the section lying west of the eastern cordillera of the Andes—and the Oriente. Practically the whole civilized and economic life of the country is situated in the small section west of this range of the Andes. East of the Andes lies the vast undeveloped territory of the Oriente. The boundaries of this region are constantly in dispute, as Ecuador and Peru have conflicting claims to a large portion of the territory. A glance at the map will show that an arm of Peru sweeps around the eastern and northeastern sides of Ecuador up to Colombia, which borders Ecuador on the north. Only a few trails cross the Andes from the settled part of Ecuador to the "Wild East"; while Peru has access to the Oriente by navigable streams. Ecuador, therefore, has been hard pressed to maintain her military forces and hence her control of the territory.

The total area under dispute is in the neighborhood of 200,000 square miles. Should Ecuador be deprived of this, she would be confined to the Andean region, the Pacific littoral, and the Galapagos Islands, amounting to approximately 75,000 square miles. More than this, she would lose her eastern outlets to the Amazon and the Atlantic Ocean via the rivers of the Oriente.

The whole question of the boundary is a complicated one hinging on old Spanish laws and decrees antedating Ecuador's independence from Spain in 1822 and from Colombia in 1830.

Although the official language of Ecuador is Spanish, which is spoken by the inhabitants of the cities and practically all portions of the country from the coastal district to the Andes, yet throughout the northern part of the Oriente district the language in general use is Quechua, the language of the Incas.

Few of the civilized or semi-civilized Indians speak or understand any other tongue; and the cholos, or mixed-bloods, as well as the ranchers, settlers, and others of Spanish descent, are obliged to speak Quechua in order to deal with the natives.

As a result it is almost impossible to conduct any explorations or other work in this portion of the Republic unless one speaks Quechua or employs interpreters.

In many respects Quechua is one of the most remarkable of all languages. Both its origin and its history are of great interest, for it was the official and universal tongue of the Inca Empire and was devised and perfected by the Incas.

In that vast Empire, which extended at its height from what is now northern Chile to the Colombian border—an area of some 380,000 square miles, with a population of nearly twenty million people embracing innumerable tribes and races, each with its own language or dialect, a common medium of understanding was most essential. To meet this the Quechua language developed.

The Oriente of Ecuador, the antithesis of the pleasant civilized zones, is a vast jungle country through which no roads pass, its great rivers being the only present means of travel. To step but a pace from their banks is to encounter dense tangled forests, seldom penetrated by white men, which resist one's passage to an almost indescribable extent.

To travel from one civilized point or river valley to another, maybe only a few miles distant in a straight line, can present an arduous journey of many days through regions either uninhabited or peopled only by Indians. Today most of these Indians are friendly, but in a few cases, such as that of the Ssabelas, who dwell between the Curaray and Napo rivers, they are extremely hostile towards any intrusion on the part of both white men and other Indian tribes. It is by means of the rivers, therefore, that the first steps towards the development of the Oriente have been taken.

In the Oriente district, as throughout the jungle country of South America, the Indians invariably live or camp close to the rivers. Their entire lives center about the streams, which control all their activities and affect the development of the tribe. Without a river they would be almost helpless, for its waters supply them with fish and turtles, it affords the easiest and quickest means of transportation and enables them to make long journeys with loads which they could never pack on their backs.

Most important of all, perhaps, is the fact that game is always most abundant near the streams, where many wild animals come to drink or to feed; while, in addition, the best timber and the most useful palms are found in the vicinity of the rivers. Finally, the alluvial lands close to the streams are the most fertile and afford the best land for cultivating maize, manioc, plantains, and other food plants. Even when traveling through the jungle across country, the Indians invariably time their day's trek so they will arrive at a camping place near a stream before darkness overtakes them.

Until recently very little has been known of the Curaray River. In fact, only a few years ago it was believed by such authorities as Richard Spruce to rise in the Llanganatis Mountains. In reality there are at least two transverse river valleys, flowing northwards, between the Llanganatis and the Curaray's head-waters.

The other natural difficulty is to reach the Oriente and the head of the Curaray, across the great mountain barrier of the Andes, of which the Llanganatis Mountains form a part. These are so formidable that at present they prevent direct communication between the river and the civilized center along the railroads. Such trails as do exist skirt these mountains, one to the north, another to the south of the obstruction. The trail to the north is open for mule transport, but that to the south is only suitable for the passage of human beings, or at best, during the dry season, for slow-moving bullocks.

Incredible as it may seem, we learned from studying the terrain as we worked our way along that it would not be very difficult to construct an automobile road to the high, eastern rim of the mountains, which could then be reached in a couple of hours from Ambato on the railroad. A fair amount of blasting to make passageways through those desperate "noses" or precipices over which I had to climb would make it possible to link up the intervening flats into a perfectly adequate mule trail into the western fringe of the Oriente traversable in one day. The work necessary to do this is by no means beyond the capacity of a country like Ecuador, which has battled geographic difficulties throughout her long history.

A new and direct passageway, supplemented by an air route, through these mountains in conjunction with the Curaray would offer a superior new line of communication between the civilized centers through the heart of the Oriente to the eastern frontier. It is hoped, therefore, that the exploration and mapping of the Curaray River and the frontier done by the Expedition will assist in the future development and opening up of this vast hinterland.

Our route had to follow the flats along the river banks during most of the journey through the mountains. The rivers wind around the ends of ridges which almost intermesh like the cogs of two gigantic gears. Wherever the cog, so to speak, ended in a sheer cliff directly on the river, we had to find a path up over the ridge, climbing usually many hundreds of feet above the river, and then we had to go down the other side to reach the valley floor again. Most of the time these ridges were very narrow, and we would come back to the valley only a few hundred yards ahead of where we had left it. By blasting a cut around the end of these spurs, river flats could very easily be linked up into a roadway. The construction of this new and direct route between the civilized part of Ecuador and the great Oriente will open up this rich but undeveloped territory to the world. The Curaray River route to the east and the land and air route to the west assure the eventual economic development of this rich region.

Throughout the Oriente, timber, of course, abounds and is utilized by the Indians for many and varied purposes. There grows the llanchama tree, from the bark of which they obtain their cloth. In preparing the cloth the tree is first ringed in two places, and the intervening bark is then stripped from the tree. The outer surface is easily peeled off, leaving a fibrous inner bark. This inner sheet is next removed and placed over a balsa log or similar object supported on trestles and is beaten with special hammers or wooden mallets, the heads of which are criss-crossed in order to grip the surface of the bark. By beating the fibrous material first one way and then another, almost any desired shape, length, or breadth may be obtained. Finally it is thoroughly washed and dried. The resultant sheet is soft, flexible, very strong and durable, and wears well. It is waterproof to a considerable degree, will not stretch when wet, and may be laundered repeatedly.

When first prepared, the bark cloth is dull grayish, but it may be bleached to snowy whiteness. The thickness of the cloth can be varied by separating the layers of the fibers and may be as thick and heavy as canvas or as thin and delicate as the finest lace. This material is often dyed or, when used by Indians, painted in various designs and colors.

Among the Zaparo Indians blankets of this material were extensively used. This is identical with the "lace-bark tree" of various portions of South and Central American and some of the West Indian islands. In Central America it is employed for making rope, for light rugs and blankets, for women's garments, and various other purposes. In Panama this bark cloth is used for making the weird costumes worn by the devil dancers during their ceremonies. It was, I believe, in use by the Incan and pre-Incan races; and bark-cloth wrappings and garments, often beautifully dyed or painted, are frequently found in the ancient graves of these people.

There are other economic plants which are worth mentioning. The most important among these are the following:

PITA. The plant resembles a large pineapple and reaches a height of eight feet or more. The leaves, which are long and blade-like, are beaten and the pulp separated from the fibers, which are very strong and durable. These are used for making nets, fish lines, bow strings, etc. It is also cultivated and grows much larger than when wild.

CHAMBIRA (Palm). A large palm tree with fibrous leaves from which the Indians obtain a soft tough "wool," as it is called, which is durable and lasts for a long time. By removing the winter covering of the old leaves, the fiber known as "chambira wool" is obtained. The young leaves, entire, were used by the Zaparo Indians for making knotless hammocks, famous in the Oriente. The "wool" itself is spun into thread and is woven into fish nets, etc. The wood is of little use and is so full of spines that it is very hard to work.

TARAPUTU (Palm). A tall palm with no spines. Very rugged, unsymmetrical head with two rows of thick, broad leaves continuous along the entire frond.

The ends of the fronds are usually broken squarely off, probably by the wind. The leaves also are very brittle. The palm is apt to end in a long "spike" extending high above. This is a very common palm along the entire trail from Indyllama down to the Villano River and on the first part of the Curaray below Puerto Tunghurahua.

The wood is hard and is used as supports for houses, cross poles on rafts, general building purposes, handles for axes, harpoons, etc. It is excellent for anything requiring a hard, durable wood. It also makes good fuel.

The leaves of the tree are employed as thatching for roofs of houses in districts where toquilla or other better leaves are not obtainable; but, as the taraputu leaves dry up and split into shreds very soon, they are very poor thatch. The young leaf-bud, or "cabbage," is very good, however. These are called yuyu in Quechua or palmites in Spanish and are widely used as salads, etc.

The taraputu is one of the hardest and darkest of all the palms of the Oriente and contains more wood in proportion to the pith than any others. Some of the old taraputu palms are so hard that an axe may be broken on them.

SHIMBI (Palm). This palm looks much like a taraputu and like the latter has no spines, but as a rule it is a smaller tree than the taraputu. It is distinguished by having four rows of leaves on each frond instead of two. The wood is not so hard as that of the taraputu. We first saw these palms on the Nashino River, where no true taraputu palms were observed.

KILI (Palms). Another spineless palm tree which somewhat resembles the true taraputu. The leaves, however, are narrower; and the ends of the fronds are seldom broken squarely off. The timber, although inferior to that of the taraputu, is used for the same purposes. It is easily recognized by its lighter weight and paler color. On the other hand, the leaves are much superior to those of the taraputu for thatching roofs, as they do not split up when dry and exposed to the sun. These palms usually grow most abundantly in hilly country and are the bushman's sign that he is approaching the hills. Many of these trees were seen near Mera.

RAMUS (Palm). This variety has very bad, flat spines. It is a thick, stunted tree with scarcely any trunk. Its head appears to grow directly from the earth. The ramus grows in clusters, the several individual trees being so close together that the entire bunch appears to be a single tree. The wood is not used for any purpose, but the leaves, which are very long and placed close together like the teeth of a comb, are used for lacing together the toquilla leaves when making the best type of thatched roof. These palms are abundant on the upper Curaray, the Villano, and the Bobonaza Rivers.

TAGUA, YARINA (Ivory Nut Palm). In general appearance it is much like the ramus, but is smaller and grows singly, not in clusters. The nuts are of great commercial value. No other portion of this palm is used. We found it growing on the upper Curaray, the Villano, and the Bobonaza Rivers.

TREMENTINA. In addition to the chincona, sarsaparilla, rhubarb, and other well-known medicinal plants, trees, and barks, the Indians of the Oriente use various little-known "herb" medicines for curing numerous diseases, injuries, insect bites, etc. Among these is the trementina tree, which has a sap with the odor of Sloan's Liniment and which is fully as efficacious as that well-known preparation.

JANDIA CARACHA. Another valuable medicinal tree with a sap which is said to be most efficacious as a cure for pyorrhea.

SHIQUARA. The oil extracted from the fruits of this tree is widely used as an ointment and to alleviate swellings and pain.

MALICAHUA. This medicinal plant is related to the flowering shrub known to the Spanish-speaking people as "Florapendula." When under the influence of the drug, a person's heart ceases to palpitate, as far as detectable by ordinary means; the whole body turns icy cold and the subject remains in an insensible state, apparently dead, for as much as twenty-four hours. It seems to have no after-effects and does not endanger life. It is, I believe, the most powerful narcotic known to the Oriente. Delicate operations may be performed upon a person while under the influence of the drug.

In preparing this the roots of the plant are washed,

the outer covering or bark is scraped off, and the remaining root is grated and pressed in a cloth. The liquid thus obtained is the narcotic, one gram of which is a full dose for any one person.

Also to be found are the Redwood, Cedar, Balsa, or Corkwood, Cinnamon, Rubber, and the "milk" or "cow" tree. None of these last were observed near Napo, but they occur on the lower portions of the Napo River and along the upper Amazon. The sap, obtained by tapping the tree, resembles thick milk and tastes like cow's milk. If exposed to the air, it coagulates or thickens like rubber. When it first issues from the tree, it is quite cool and very refreshing. It is said that a large tree—about three feet in diameter—will yield ten gallons of the milk-like sap. The tree also bears an edible fruit which is sweet but slightly acid and is a favorite food of monkeys and parrots. According to the natives, the tree yields far more "milk" during the full moon than at the time of the new moon.

There is also the Strychnostoxifera, from which the famous curare poison is abstracted, and the Barbasco, now becoming an article of commerce as an insecticide on account of the rotenone which it contains.

The Indians find many uses for barbasco, the most prominent being fishing. When the roots and stems are mashed up in the waters of some creek, or small river, the fish become stupefied and float helplessly down on the surface of the water to be caught in prepared traps made of wild cane. Though this poison is fatal to fish, insects, and other lower forms of life, it does not seem to have any affect on human beings when consumed in the relatively weak dilution in which it is found in the poisoned fish.

Ecuador, in general, is a country rich in natural resources, the majority of which have as yet been but little developed. Only near the coast and along the railroads, highways, and civilized tablelands have these been exploited. Ecuador is a land of astonishing beauty and one with a fascinating history. With its great variety of immense jungles, extensive rivers, lofty mountains, volcanoes, cataracts, quaint old-world cities, and high, picturesque tablelands, it offers a variety of scenery and interesting contrasts that are seldom seen elsewhere.

Within its limits can be found almost any desired climate known to the world. Along the coast and in the far Oriente it is hot and tropical. In the highlands or tablelands, however, the climate is that of a perpetual springtime; while still higher one may reach a frigid climate of everlasting snow and ice.

There are vast areas of rich farm and grazing lands, immense areas of forest filled with valuable timber trees, rubber, medicinal plants, and other forest products. Only a few of the country's mineral resources are being developed. With the exception of one sound and well-established company, the bulk of the gold is washed by the Indians with the crudest of appliances from the beds of the rivers.

Even before the land now included in the Republic of Ecuador had come under Incan dominion, some of the native races mined, smelted, and worked copper, silver, and gold to a considerable degree.

In some respects the gold work of the Ecuadorean tribes far excelled that of any other of the American races, and much of the finest gold work of ancient Peru originated in Quitu, as Ecuador was then called. Indeed, some of the old Ecuadorean gold work is absolutely amazing. In the vicinity of Manabí and Esmeraldas on the Pacific Coast archeologists have unearthed quantities of gold beads so small as to be unrecognizable as such when viewed by the unaided eye. Many of these are smaller than the head of a common pin and look like mere grains or tiny nuggets of gold. But when examined through a lens they are revealed as handmade beads, not only pierced but often elaborately carved or embossed, and quite frequently composed of a number of pieces of gold welded or soldered together to produce a single bead.

When Spain conquered the Inca Empire there was probably as much gold in the form of bullion, utensils, and ornaments as in all the European countries combined—some say far more. Although largely confined to the nobility and priesthood, yet there was no law against the use of gold by others. It is not unusual to find mummies of ordinary members of the community, such as artisans, husbandmen, etc., with golden ornaments upon the desiccated bodies or beside them in the graves.

At present the world is scrambling for natural resources. Few other places in the world offer more promising business opportunities than in Ecuador. All that is needed is moderate capital to carry on until a stretch of land is cleared and crops are marketable. In the Oriente the settler has before him thousands of square miles of untouched territory adapted to almost any form of agriculture or stock raising if a careful selection is made. To this he is given every help by the government.

The delayed development of the natural resources of Ecuador is largely due to the natural geographical and topographical obstacles with which she has to contend, and the consequent difficulties of transportation. But these conditions are being gradually overcome. The unlimited openings for establishing factories and new industries should rapidly stimulate a flow of capital into the country and lead to speedy development.

Appendix C

LIST OF ORNITHOLOGICAL SPECIMENS
COLLECTED
BY THE ANDES-AMAZON EXPEDITION
AS CLASSIFIED BY THE AMERICAN MUSEUM
OF NATURAL HISTORY
1935-6-7

1935-6-7.

1 Crypturus macconnelli fumosus
1 Egretta candidissima
1 Florida caerulea
8 Ibyctes carunculatus
1 Micrastur melanoleucus buckleyi
1 Asturina nitido nitido
2 Geranoaetus melanoleucus
4 Buteo poecilochrous
1 Buteo p. platypterus
3 Falco sparverius
2 Chamaepetes goudoti tschudii
1 Penelope montaguii brooki
2 Penelope j. jacquacu
1 Pipile c. cumanensis

2	Opisthocomus hoazin
1	Psophia napensis
1	Ionornis martinica
1	Columba albilinea
2	Zenaida auriculata hypoleuca
4	Metriopelia melanoptera saturatior
1	Chamaepelia passerina quitensis
1	Larus serranus
5	Attagis latreillii
2	Gallinago jamesoni
2	Merganetta armata
2	Oxyura ferruginea
1	Ara serera castaneifrons
1	Amazona festiva
2	Pionus chalcopterus
2	Piaya cayana mesura
2	Crotophaga ani
1	Bubo virginianus nigrescene
1	Asio stygius
1	Speotyto cunicularia nanodes
1	Glaucidium jardinii
1	Stealornis caripensis
1	Nyctiphrynus
3	Pharomachrus a. auriceps
3	Pharomachrus auriceps heliactrii
2	Trogonurus personatus personatus
4	Momotus aeq. aequatorialis
1	Ceryle amazona
2	Galbula melanogenia
1	Galbalcyrhynchus leucotis
1	Notharcus h. hyperrhynchus
1	Nonnula brunnea

1   Monasa flavirostris
1   Monasa nigrifons
1   Semnornis ramphastinus
3   Capito richardsoni
1   Campephilus pollens pollens
1   Phloeoceastes melanoleucos
2   Hypanthus rivolii brevirostris
2   Tripsurus p. pucherani
1   Celeus grammicus
2   Ramphastas swainsoni
1   Ramphastas cuvieri
2   Pteroglossus pluricinctus
1   Pteroglossus erythropygius
3   Aulacarhynchus a. albivitta
2   Andigena nigrirostris spilorhynchus
2   Andigena laminirostris
1   Threnetes cervinicauda
2   Doryfera johannae
1   Phoethornis strigularis subrufescens
2   Phoethornis griseogularis
2   Phoethornis superciliosus moorei
2   Phoethornis guyi emiliae
2   Campylopterus obscuru aequatorialis
1   Campylopterus villavicencio
1   Florisuca mellivora mellivora
2   Amizilia tzacatl jucunda
3   Chrysuronia oeone oeone
4   Chlorostilbon m. melanorhynchus
2   Thalurania nigrifasciata
3   Colibri iolata
1   Colibri delphinae
3   Oriotrochilus chimborazo jamesoni

2 Urochroa bougueri leucura
2 Heliodoxa leadbeateri
2 Ionolaima schreibersii
1 Helianthea coeligena columbiana
1 Helianthea torquata
1 Helianthea fulgidigula
1 Helianthea lutetiae
2 Pterophanes cyanopterus
1 Lafresnayea lafresnayi gayi
2 Aglaeactes cup. cupripennis
1 Boissonneaua mattewsi
2 Boissonneaua flavescens tinochlora
2 Vestipedes nigrioestis
3 Vestipedes luciani
1 Ocreatus cissiurus
2 Adelomyia m. melanogenys
2 Phlogophilus hemileucurus
1 Urosticte ruficrissa
1 Heliangelus strophianus
2 Metallura tyriantheria quitensis
1 Chalcostigma herrani
6 Chalcostigma stanleyi stanleyi
1 Ramphomicron m. microhynchum
5 Lesbia victoriae aequatorialis
4 Popelairia popelairii
4 Chaetocercus mulsanti
1 Xiphocolaptes promeropirhynchus ignotus
2 Xiphorhynchus t. triangularis
3 Lepidocolaptes lacrymiger aequatorialis
1 Pseudocolaptes boissonneauti orientalis
1 Dendrocincla lafresnayei ridgwayi
1 Sclerurus caudacutus brunneus

1   Philydor erythropterus
1   Philydor erythrocercus subfulvus
1   Automolus ochrolaemus turdinus
1   Automolus rubiginosus brunnescens
1   Hyloctistes subulatus subulatus
3   Asthenes f. flammulata
1   Margarornis perlata
1   Xenops rutilans heterurus
1   Cranioleuca guttata peruviana
1   Synallaxis azarae media
3   Schizoeca griseo-murina
3   Upucerthia excelsior excelsior
2   Grallaria gigantea
1   Grallaria squamigeria
2   Grallaria r. ruficapilla
2   Grallaria monticola
1   Grallaria rufila rufila
1   Cymbilaimus lineatus intermedius
1   Myrmeciza immaculatus berlepschi
1   Drymophila c. caudata
1   Hylophylax naevia
1   Conopophaga aurita occidentalis
1   Scytalopus latrans
1   Pipra erythrocephala berlepschi
1   Teleonema filicauda
1   Masius corunulatus
1   Chloropipo h. holochora
2   Pipreola jacunda
1   Euchlornis
1   Ampelion rubricristata
1   Ampelioides tschudii
2   Cotinga cayana

3 Cotinga mayana
2 Querula purpurata
2 Cephalopterus ornatus
6 Rupicola sanguinolenta
5 Rupicola peruviana aequatorialis
1 Agriornis s. solitaria
3 Cnemarchus erythropygius
1 Muscisaxicola alpina
1 Octhoeca fumicolor brunneifrons
2 Poecilotriccus ruficeps aequatorialis
1 Spizitornis parulus aequatorialis
1 Mecocerculus s. stidopterus
3 Pyrrhonyias cinnamomea pyrrhoptera
2 Pyrocephalus rubinus
1 Elaenia gigas
1 Pitangus s. sulphuratus
1 Tyrannus m. melancholicus
2 Myiozetetes cayanensis hellmayri
1 Cyanocorax violaceus
4 Xanthoura yncas yncas
1 Cinclus leuconotus
1 Cinnicerthia unibrunnea
1 Leucolepis arada salvini
1 Henicorhina l. leucophrys
3 Cistothorus platensis aequatorialis
2 Turdus fuscater gigantodes
2 Turdus chiguanco Chiquanco
1 Hylocichla ustulata swainsoni
1 Pachysylvia ochraceiceps ferrugineifrons
1 Dendroica fusca
1 Myiothlypis nigrocristatus
2 Myioborus bairdi

1   Conirostrum s. sitticolor
1   Conirostrum fraseri
1   Diglossa pa. personata
1   Diglossa lafresnayei
1   Diglossa aterrima
1   Diglossa albilatera
3   Cholorophanes spiza caerulescens
2   Dacnis cayano glaucogularis
1   Dacnis lineata
3   Tangara arthus goodsoni
1   Tangara arthus aequatorialis
3   Tangara schrankii
1   Tangara syanicollis caeruleocephala
1   Tangara cyanicollis cyanopygia
1   Tangara n. nigro-cincta
2   Tangara xanthocephala venusta
1   Tangara gyrola nupera
3   Tangara p. parzudakii
3   Tangara chilensis
1   Tangara atricapilla-heinei
3   Tangara xanthogastra
1   Chlorochrysa phoenicotis
1   Tanagra c. chrysopasta
1   Tanagra xanthogaster brevirostris
1   Thraupis palmarum violilavata
5   Thraupis episcopus quaesita
1   Thraupis bonariensis darwini
2   Pamphocelus icteronotus
1   Pamphocelus nigrogularis
1   Tachyphonus delatrii
2   Buthraupis c. cucullata
2   Compsocoma somtuosa beazae

2   Psittospiza r. riefferi
2   Cissopis l. leveriana
1   Sicalis luteiventris
1   Catemenia inornata
4   Phrygilus unicolor grandis
2   Arremon spectabilis
1   Idiospiza homochroa
1   Sporophila luctuosa
1   Hedymeles ludoviciana
1   Allopetes pallidinuchus pafallactae
1   Allopetes schistaceus
3   Pheucticus crissalis
1   Arremonops conirostris chrysoma
2   Cacicus cela
3   Cacicus u. uropygialis
1   Amblycercus solitarius
2   Archiplanus leucorhamphus
1   Molothrus bonariensis
1   Zarhynchus wagleri wagleri
1   Ostinops d. decumanus
1   Ostinops alfredi atrocastaneus
2   Ostinops augustifrons
3   Pezites militaris bellicosa

Appendix D

MAMMALS

COLLECTED BY

THE EXPEDITION

Number

2 Highland (hairy) Tapir (from an altitude of 14,000 feet.)

3 Spectacled Bears (from Llanganatis Mts., 12,000 feet, Andes)

1 Pudu (pigmy deer)

3 Andean Wolf-fox

6 Gray Deer (Odocoileus)

2 Brocket Deer (Mazuma)

3 Marmosets

1 Skunk

2 Opossums

1 Porcupine

1 Titi Monkey

1 Nine-banded Armadillo

2 Coatis

12 Bats

Number

1   Ocelot
2   Otters
2   Two-toed Sloths

The mammal collection is limited in comparison with the ornithological one because the Expedition sought to collect primarily only three of the above species: hairy tapir, bear, and wolf, the Andean varieties of which are practically unrepresented in the museums and zoological societies of the United States. The pudu or pigmy deer especially, is believed to be extremely rare. No special effort was made to collect the remainder. They fell more or less haphazardly to our hunting.

The bird life of Ecuador and Peru is remarkable; and, although collectors of considerable note have been drawn to these regions on account of it, there are still many rare specimens that have never been acquired. For this reason we concentrated our zoological effort on obtaining as complete as possible an ornithological collection.